Volume 3: Sidelined

Decisions Decisions: Getting Answers to Life's Challenges   Large Print

Haneefa Mateen

Copyright © 2023 by Haneefa Mateen

All rights reserved.

ISBN 978-1-73772-19-6-3

No portion of this book may be reproduced in any form without written permission from the publisher or author, except as permitted by U.S. copyright law.

Disclaimer: The author of this book, Volume 3: Sidelined: Decisions, Decisions' stories, experiences and opinions are from author's perspective and are not intended as medical advice or the use of any techniques as a form of treatment for physical, medical, psychiatric, mental health problems either directly or indirectly. The intent of the author is only to share experiences in a general nature in her quest for emotional and spiritual wellbeing. In the event that you use any of the information in this book for yourself, which is your constitutional right, the author and publisher assumes no responsibility or liability whatsoever for readers or purchasers of this book.

Volume 3: Sidelined is a non-fiction story, however some names, locations, and other identifying information were changed to protect privacy of individuals.

Book Cover art: Haneefa Mateen

Contents

Introduction	1
PART ONE HEALTH	9
Chapter 1: Geb Health	10
Chapter 2: Medical I Ching	22
Chapter 3: Would You Want to Live to be 100?	29
Chapter 4: What are Medical Specialists for?	34
Chapter 5: Prognosis	45
Chapter 6: Another Before My Time	74

PART TWO: LIFE USING A WHEELCHAIR	82
Chapter 7: Getting a Wheelchair	83
Chapter 8: Not for the Faint of Heart	94
Chapter 9: Trains	100
Chapter 10: Paratransit Services	105
Chapter 11: By Air	112
Chapter 12: Invisible	116
Chapter 13: Wheelchair Coming On!	122
Chapter 14: University	126
Chapter 15: University: Tarot Card Guidance	141
Chapter 16: University: Triquetra Spread	147

Chapter 17: University: Personal Reflections on the Meaning	154
Chapter 18: University: The Squeaky Wheel	169
Chapter 19: What if There is a Fire?	181
Chapter 20: Elevators Out	189
PART THREE: HEALING	207
Chapter 21: Other Aspects of Auset	208
Chapter 22: Be Careful What You Ask For	218
Chapter 23: Mother Mary in Africa	226
Chapter 24 Wisdom Gained	231
Books and Articles	235
1. Author's Bio	243

Introduction

People ask me, "How did you, and still do, go through tough life challenges, such as illness that led to using a wheelchair, and can smile?" They want to know what I did to survive and keep going. Divination is one of the tools I use.

No need to suffer depression and anxiety worrying what decisions to make, or did you make the right decision. Is it even your decision to make or someone else's? No need to worry what is going to happen in the future, because your guides give you insight into the situation, you are concerned about, and will show you what you have control over and what you don't. Depression and fears often comes from feeling trapped or stuck. Asking for higher guidance for what you can do to improve your situation, through the use of divination gives you solutions and putting that guidance into action, gets you unstuck. It does take faith and courage because what you will be shown is new and different. Or often what you've known all along you need to do.

"Insanity is doing the same thing over and over again and expecting different results." Albert Einstein

Fear of change or what others will think, may have stopped you. Divination gives you encouragement by showing you options. The results often better than you could have ever imagined. Miracles, lots of miracles and abundance happen.

When you start to see less crises in your life, as you understand how the universe functions around you, and make better choices in your thoughts and behaviors, then it is not hard, even for us who are hardheaded, to believe. Especially when your life begins to flow smoothly synchronically, and what you need simply shows up abundantly. Divination provides roadmaps or a GPS that lets you know where the traffic congestion is and guides you through the detours. Sometimes we get stuck in traffic anyway. GPS gives alerts and warnings ahead of time. Divination also gives you alerts and can help you get back on the main road of your life.

It decreases conflicts in relationships by allowing the oracle to show us what's best. From your heart with sincerity, you can ask the following questions: How do I improve myself to have better friendships? Should I share or not? Am I enabling? Or do I tend to be selfish and not know how to share and love? Show me how to feel love and receive love. How do I get along with his or her family? Should we buy this car at this time and from what dealer? Or change employment? Or relocate? Where do I go for guidance when I'm feeling sad or frustrated? If we disagree on what to do, what is best for the whole situation? What prayers do we need for healing? And then follow the guidance, each step of the way. Relationships help us learn, grow and change.

This is not a religious book. I use some foreign language terms because that is the way I learned them and is my way of continuing to honor these indigenous cultures and beliefs. With deep respect for indigenous cultures and the people who truly have the knowledge, I thank them and yield to them.

Religions and holy scriptures threaten human beings with damnation and going to hell for our transgressions, yet doesn't tell or show us <u>how</u> to stay out of hell. Just, "don't this or don't do that," with contradictory messages of "we were born in sin," "confess and you'll be forgiven," and don't let the devil tempt you." To be honest, I've tried and tried to understand the Bible and Quran translated into old English, with stories I can't relate to our current days and times. Religious leaders argue over the meanings. The use of oracles and other forms of divination can show each of us, as well as our communities how to stay out of unnecessary hell in both this life (and the next).

Hopefully this book introduces you to different perspectives as my personal stories bring understanding of how ancient and now popularized practices for making decisions — when used properly — brings improved quality of life, inner peace, satisfaction, and sense of purpose. And is inspirational to you on your own life's journey.

In the first book, <u>Mother's Love from Beyond</u>, readers learned about my childhood and early adult years, as I was prepared through life experiences to accept that there are many different ways of healing and knowing. Readers gained faith and courage along with me as I learned to trust intuitive higher guidance. In this book, I offer tools for you gaining access to your own guidance for your own life, while continuing with my stories from Volume 1 and Volume 2, of Decisions Decisions of how I was introduced to these divination tools and how my lifestyle changed along the way. This book is mostly written in the order I learned these techniques however, the stories are updated with my current thoughts, events, and style of writing. Previous readers asked me to go into more details about my middle years, my thirties, forties, and early fifties to explain how I got from, and transformed beyond multiple crises and obstacles I endured described in Volume 2, from then to now.

My goal with this book, Decisions Decisions, as with my other books in the "Spirituality Made Simple series" is to make spirituality and healing simple. Simple to understand, and simple to apply to daily life. I use several approaches to meet different readers' needs, interests, and learning styles. Some people learn best from information and research. Other people enjoy and learn from life stories as examples. Here, both approaches are combined. Take what you need and leave the rest. At different times later in your life you may want to come back to this series for more understanding.

PART ONE HEALTH

Chapter 1: Geb Health

Remember the first career reading (in Volume 1, Chapter 1) that I did back in 1993? Metu Neter cards: Geb tem tchaas/Amen hetep. I Ching hexagram 40 Deliverance (lines 2, 3, 5, and 6) into hexagram 33 Retreat? Well, Geb represents our health or the health of a situation. In my case, Geb tem definitely was about to mean declining health, and a retreat from my career.

There was something about severe crushing, sharp ice pick stabbing, breathtaking chest pains and fatigue for the years 1995 through 1996, without doctors knowing what was wrong, would make anyone think they were going to die. It made me change my priorities in life. That's how I decided to go off to college and then to Africa. It would be a once in a lifetime deal. Just like my 87-year-old grandmother wanting to see the Western United States before she died. That was in 1992, and she was still living nearly two decades later. Therefore I do not regret my decision to go.

Prior to me going to Zimbabwe, I began to get up early in the morning and do grounding exercises with Tai Chi and aligning my hara line (from the book, Light Emerging) and making my intention of being fully present in the Earth plane throughout the day. After all, how could I heal if I wasn't giving my body a live message?

Starting my morning aligning my hara line did help. This visualization seemed to make my whole day flow easily along with a positive mood. Definitely felt different on the days when I forgot or wasn't able to start my day that way. Similar happened if I stayed up during the night, I felt detached. Afraid to be fully present in the physical but I made my vow to do so anyway, after four years of religiously meditating twice a day and being a strict vegan had made me feel alone and spacey. I made this commitment to be more grounded after I realized that my health was probably falling apart, as well as the rest of my life, because I had gotten angry at my ex-husbands and roommates and told God that I didn't want to have anything anymore, because people used me for my money and my talents and frequently took away what I worked very hard to earn. Well, God answered my prayers. Now I, had to find a way to convince God to reverse my request.

Going to the School for International Training in Vermont and then on to Zimbabwe was a blessing, and I temporarily had some of my health restored. Although I no longer had the constant chest pains, there were a few warnings signs while I was on the college campus that all was not well. Occasionally I struggled to climb stairs and lost control of my bladder. In Zimbabwe, my menstrual bleeding was heavy, and I had terrible headaches which probably meant I was anemic.

Several months after being back in the United States, lab tests showed a different kind of anemia. My mean corpuscle volume (MCV) was high, indicating that my red blood cells were too large. Megaloblastic macrocytic anemia causes too few red blood cells, not enough oxygen, with symptoms of shortness of breath, tingling, burning and weakness in arms and legs with difficulty walking, high irregular heart rate with risk of heart failure, mood changes of depression, anxiety and confusion. I had all of these symptoms and had told the doctors that I had been a strict vegan for ten years. All of my blood work was usually just inside the border of the lowest normal range. Therefore, doctors frequently ignored my test results as not significant although I had severe symptoms affecting my daily functioning. Perhaps the reason other people who are vegan can get away without it affecting their health, is because they don't have celiac disease, gastritis, or Crohn's disease, that I was later diagnosed with that interferes with absorption of food like what happened to me.

Getting Medical Care

While I was homeless, I began to hate going to case managers, including Tim who was one of my favorite case managers, for making promises about how the system is going to help me. Built my dreams and hopes up only to have them torn down again and again. The case managers were excited about "money coming" to me, but that doesn't mean much to me without my health and ability to care for my needs. It was very difficult for me to even want anything anymore. Reality of being poor and homeless got shoved in my face day after day.

It felt like I was in a very desperate situation that I had not the faintest idea how to resolve myself, so I was forced to ask for help and depend on others. This perceived desperation made me impatient, although I had been patient with most previous life challenges. It's hard to have patience when appointments with doctors and Social Security offices are months apart.

They smile and say, "That's the way the system is. You just have to wait." Or, "it's only one month's wait. Usually it takes two or three months or even two years!"

But of course, I didn't want to hear that. I was in constant pain, exhausted and had depression because of the excessive waiting, and being unemployment with loss of friends and social status. My whole life was on hold.

The case managers seemed to not have done their homework. It was very hard to get a straight answer from anyone. They hadn't the faintest idea. Yet, while I waited for what may or may not happen from public benefits, they wanted me to continue pretending with them that everything was okay, and they were helping me. I had to sign their paperwork, so they get paid biweekly, while I waited over a year for money and medical benefits. Same with doctors, they didn't have to do anything for me, just treat me like a specimen so they can get their degrees and move on. Yet they wouldn't fill out the papers so I could get my medical card, so I too could move on.

As you can tell, I was very frustrated because without a medical card for a whole year, the doctors weren't able to do the necessary expensive tests like computerized tomography (CAT) scans or magnetic resonance images (MRIs) and blood tests to help them know what was wrong with me, to have an accurate diagnosis to give me medicine and treatment.

Tim did refer me to a disability lawyer after social security denied me three times during a year of me trying to go through the application process alone. The lawyer worked behind the scenes gathering my medical records, to put together a case. After a successful court hearing with a female judge, they approved me to receive Social Security disability income and benefits. I cried when I read the award letter because it described me in a way I wouldn't ever want to be.

Trying to get medical help so that I could get my life back became my main focus. I was angry that the pain and fatigue made me so tired that I could not think straight, which then made me irritable and forgetful. This made me feel irresponsible, lazy, and confused.

One day, I suddenly I realized I left my Social Security award letter with a case manager, whom I hoped kept it safe. I was feeling very trapped inside with the unpredictability of my illness and the weather. The weatherman forecasted "only a dusting of snow" but there was enough to shovel! I needed my Social Security award letter when I was to go to the doctor on the following Monday.

I had to figure out how to get around in the snow, since walking was difficult for me and I didn't drive or have a car. I had planned a straight bus route, now I would have to take a detour. It would've been better if I had a bus pass then I wouldn't had to worry about how long my bus transfer card would last. I didn't have a bus pass because of the confusion about when my social security benefits would arrive.

I desperately needed groceries too. Some of my depression was from not eating enough, which then kept me awake at night, without sleep I was too tired to cook, or wash dishes and it became a vicious cycle. Public aid cut my food stamps and cash because my original Social Security award letter from the court decision made back in November stated that I would receive benefits through January. However, public aid only gave me cash for two months. I thought this would include getting a January check and food stamps, but it didn't. So there went my budget. Add snow to no money, and difficulty getting around, and you have a big feeling of being trapped with always having to wait.

Chapter 2: Medical I Ching

Destiny reading hexagram 34 (lines 3 and 6) into hexagram 38.

According to The Medical I Ching, hexagram 38 indicates sudden onset and rapid progress of diseases, but prognosis is fair for recovery in the end. Since there are contradictory symptoms, may experience negligence from medical doctors giving wrong diagnoses or prescriptions.

As you'll read in both my memoirs, doctors frequently misdiagnosed me resulting in me almost dying at least three times — first from an ectopic pregnancy, the other times from septic infections, probably from undiagnosed endometriosis, caught just in time. Each time I was in the hospital for several days before doctors decided to do emergency exploratory surgery because they didn't know what was wrong.

After they told me what they found, I researched their diagnoses and found I had all the classic textbook symptoms! The doctors ignored my symptoms based on "nonsignificant" test results. Now, even Black women celebrities with money and good insurance say they weren't listened to and almost died during pregnancy and childbirth. More women began coming forward in 2021 and 2022, especially women of color, and telling their stories of having their pain ignored and misdiagnosed. Similar to the "me too movement", except that they're calling it "medical gaslighting." On social media and YouTube, you can hear the personal stories and read the hundreds of comments underneath.

Hexagram 34 described the earlier diseases I had with fevers, including complications of measles at five years old with pneumonia. Possible aggressive illnesses I'm not sure of because to me, perhaps because of delayed diagnoses, I thought my illnesses came on slowly. This gave doctors extra time to "save me." However, the neurologist did tell me that it was rare for even patients with multiple sclerosis's walking to decline so fast going from walker to wheelchair in four years. Muscle spasms are symptoms of neuromuscular diseases. Line 3 can have lung problems like I did with pneumonia. As I got older, I do 'catch cold in my lower back.' In high school, I had boils on my butt from sitting on those hard, wooden chairs. Line 6: My prognoses would be fair. Initially, doctors' prognoses were moderate to severe, but I recovered beyond their expectations. Headaches? Rarely, only whenever I had high fevers or anemia.

My lips and rosy cheeks are naturally red when I take my vitamins. Found out the hard way, that when my lips are lighter than my face, then I'm anemic. In 1999, I was having dinner with a friend but didn't have the appetite to eat. In the middle of the night, I got an awful pain in my lower belly. Afraid, remembering the other two times I had terrible belly pain, I called an ambulance to take me to the emergency room. There a white doctor examined me and checked the skin color "normal" box on the intake form. She later had a specialist reexamined me that was African American that wrote in my medical chart "skin color pale and grayish." After discharge she told me, "I'm glad the color came back in your face."

Friends noticed too and commented. I asked them, "But why didn't you tell me that before?"

I'd been going back-and-forth to doctors for two months for the cramping pain in my left back kidney area. They kept telling me my lab and x-ray results were normal. Later in the ER with terrible abdominal pain there were tiny kidney stones in my dark reddish infected urine. They kept me in the hospital for 10 days because even with IV antibiotics, the doctors had difficulty getting my fever down. They later discovered an abscess and tried a new noninvasive procedure to drain it. I improved soon after. One of the doctors told me, just before discharging me from the hospital, that he stopped the other doctors for doing major surgery on me because he was sure I would have died on the operating table. Now I faithfully drink my water and take my vitamins with iron in it.

Ever the practical one, it makes better sense to me, to solve the underlying problem than to try to cover it up. Lips dry and cracked? Drink more water. The rest of your body will thank you. Grateful that you also eat healthy nutritious foods, then your lips become naturally full and red. Perhaps men's attraction to young women with red lips is an unconscious wisdom for survival of both the woman and child throughout pregnancy and childbirth. When a woman is anemic, she is more likely to hemorrhage during childbirth. Now with lip gloss and lipstick men don't know what they're getting.

Chapter 3: Would You Want to Live to be 100?

In the book, <u>Love, Medicine and Miracles</u>, Dr.Bernie Siegel asked, "Would you want to live to be 100 years old?" When I thought about the question in 1989 and again in 1999 along with the street corner Jehovah Witnesses asking, "Wouldn't you want to live forever" my response was, why would anyone want to live forever? Especially in this mess of a world we've made!

Later I read, <u>Return of the Rishi,</u> by Deepak Chopra M.D. where he wrote that spontaneous remissions are possible with the desire of the whole person to recover completely because the body has to obey when both the doctor and the patient believes deep in their hearts that the patient can get well. Not just with restored health but also happiness. I would like the happiness, but at this point in my life I don't know if I wanted to live to be 100 or to recover completely. I did seek out answers after a doctor told me I almost died in the hospital in September 1999. I was so happy to be alive that I was silly. Then I wondered why I was so happy to be alive after wanting to die inside all year after losing my friends, my health, income, status, independence, home, etc. My life situation hadn't changed. Medical records gave me the impression that there was a strong chance that I might have ovarian cancer. I had to wait two months to get appointments and get retested. In the meantime I agonized and that's some real soul-searching. This led me back to Dr. Bernie's Siegel's other question, "If you only have one day or two weeks, six months, a year to live, how would you spend it? Certainly, you wouldn't waste it trying to please others and doing things you hate."

In one way, I feel as if I wasted a whole year and a lot of mental and physical energy worrying about my health, the healthcare system and services for the poor indigent people. It was one constant struggle. I wasn't happy most of 1999 and perhaps it's because it was easier to focus on my health than the pain of comparing the previous two years when I was in college and Africa. There I felt the happiest I ever remember being in my whole life. I was also the healthiest. Perhaps I couldn't imagine or dream of happiness and all I experienced while I was away as being possible upon return to the United States. All I remember is the pain and loneliness I had before I left.

For two decades, I struggled alone with being the first Black woman in the Air National Guard kitchen, the only Black nurse on staff, the only Black student in class, the only Black patient in therapy groups, the only one in my immediate family to complete college and become a professional. First in my family to get a divorce not only once, but twice. Having had a near death experience I saw and related to the world differently. Only one meant total self-sufficient emotionally because no one I knew understood what I was going through, and if they did they didn't say. Only and first adds up to lonely.

If I could actually choose, to be healthy again, maybe I would. When I learned to meditate, I made my own inner peace and joy. But I longed deeply for companionship and understanding from others. I cried and prayed to not be so lonely. To eventually choose to begin knocking down self-imposed barriers to possibilities of living in a supportive community with others, maybe even have a family or a mate. It would require a lot of effort.

Chapter 4: What are Medical Specialists for?

After the standard wait of two years, Social Security gave me a monthly check and Medicare benefits, then I was able to go to better hospitals and specialists. When I moved out to the suburbs my doctor's appointments and hospital care were unbelievably better. Patients were seen by the doctor within a few minutes of arrival. This was a big difference from receiving health care at Cook County hospital, or Loretto hospital with full waiting rooms and ever changing medical student doctors every time I went, sitting all day waiting to get registered, to see the doctor, for the lab tests and X-rays, then more hours to have my prescriptions filled.

A couple of my friends, and also older family members who would tell me going to Cook County Hospital and other teaching hospitals was the best, because they had up-to-date medical science. I didn't find this to be true, especially with the disrespect poor people "of color" received. Perhaps true for elders who remember a time when they spent three days in waiting rooms at Cook County hospital, while I complained of only six hours or more. Researching now as I write this book, the history of Cook County Hospital, I read that indeed it was previously the best in the United States as it implemented the new law that doctors had to have standardized training and take an exam to become doctors. Cook County hospital pioneered the first blood banks and specialized surgeries. Considering that in the 1800s hospitals didn't even exist, if you were lucky doctors made house calls, but even then medication and treatments were very few, so basically health care was limited to somebody sitting next to your bed holding your hand until you expired. This puts what the elders were trying to tell me into perspective. But back in the early 2000s, I thought I was receiving inferior care.

I grew up only knowing of having a family doctor. Therefore, I didn't know there were specialists. While I was in the hospital in 2003, after a kidney stone and endoscopies for digestive problems, the doctors brought in an infectious disease doctor, because they were wondering how come I had partial paralysis and was using a wheelchair. She asked me, "What countries have you traveled to?"

"Zimbabwe in 1997, Jamaica 1996, and Korea while in the Air Force in 1980."

"Have you been to wooded areas in the United States?"

"Yes, the college in Vermont and I frequency went camping outside in tents in the Midwest."

"We will test you for Lyme's disease, and Dengue Fever from Jamaica's mosquitoes and other diseases."

When the tests results came back, she told me, " I have to send another blood sample, on ice all the way to Texas. I spoke to a specialist there, because it's a possibility that you may have brucellosis. Brucellosis is rare in United States because we vaccinate our farm animals. It does still exist with livestock along our southern borders."

Maybe it was from trying to milk the cow in the Zimbabwe village. I didn't get symptoms immediately. It started with extreme fatigue and sleeping day and night after I returned to college in the United States. I was so tired that I will wake up take one spoonful of food, that my classmates brought to me, and fall right back to sleep. Gradually, during the next year I began to lose the use of my legs and then my arms. But it's been four years since I was in Zimbabwe.

She called me a week later excited, "I never had a patient with brucellosis before. You're my first patient with it! You're lucky to be alive. Although brucellosis is endemic in Africa if you had stayed there you probably would've died. We can treat you. These will be strong antibiotics, so we will have to monitor you closely."

I took the antibiotic for six weeks and then she sent another blood sample to the doctor in Texas and gratefully the results were negative.

I thought the infectious disease doctor was to be my new doctor. When I made another appointment with her for an unrelated minor ailment, she asked me, "Why don't you go back to the other doctor you had when you were in the hospital? She's your primary care doctor."

After the infectious disease doctor diagnosed me with brucellosis, she also referred me to the neurologist who finally gave me an additional diagnosis of spinocerebellar degeneration. He, the infectious disease doctor, and my primary care doctor were true medical detectives.

However, there can be too many other specialists with few of them communicating with each other. In 2007, A Filipino doctor who worked as a home care nurse thought I had Raynaud's Syndrome and recommended to my primary care doctor that I go to a rheumatologist specialist. He looked at my fingertips and nail beds with a small microscope and told me I did indeed have Raynaud's Syndrome. He prescribed a calcium channel blocker. When I told my cardiologist, she changed my medication to the same. With this new knowledge about how much trouble spasms of tiny capillaries can make, it occurred to me almost all my pains were from spasms: coronary artery spasms, mesentery artery spasms, urethra spasm urinary retention, interstitial cystitis with crampy bladder spasms backing urine up into my kidneys. If my specialists had talked to each other they might have figured this out amongst themselves.

Raynaud's syndrome is vasospasms or constriction of the arteries and capillaries, so the fingers turn pale white, then bluish from the lack of oxygen, then red as the fingers warm up. Rinsing my hands or food items in cold water would make my fingers throb. Drinking cold water would also give me chest pains and headaches. I hated having to dig, to get food out of the freezer. My fingers felt sore for hours, sometimes days afterwards. Raynaud's syndrome can similarly affect the feet.

I remember feeling miserable after walking five long street blocks to school when I was 10 and 11 years old. Sometimes, I would go to the school nurse. Coming from the upper mid-Atlantic states to the southern Midwest then moving to an upper Midwest state with below zero temperatures and windchill, I wasn't used to the cold. Most of the time I was without mittens and no thermal underwear. It seemed like it would take hours for me to warm up. One day I saw an index card on the nurse's desk with my name on it and the word "hypochondriac." I wondered what it meant. It may have helped if she had known about Raynaud's syndrome. But maybe not. My family was poor and probably couldn't have done anything about it anyway.

This new neurologist told me my symptoms would be like multiple sclerosis, but I didn't have multiple sclerosis. One of MS symptoms is intolerance to temperature extremes. Initially, this was predominantly with the heat outside in the summer or inside a hot room. It wasn't until 2015, that I read in a <u>Momentum</u> magazine article that people with MS can also have cold intolerance and Raynaud's phenomenon. Because neuromuscular diseases affect the autonomic nervous system, there's difficulty regulating internal body temperature to automatically sweat when too hot or shiver when we are too cold. For me, being too hot or too cold is extremely painful, and causes my arms and legs to weaken.

Chapter 5: Prognosis

It was unusually hot outside. I went inside the bank, and after standing in line for a while, when I got up to the teller's window, I had difficulty using my hands. I had to ask him to take my state ID out of my wallet for me. Usually I would be all right after being in the cold grocery store. Afterwards, on the way home and after I arrived home, I had difficulty breathing so I called my neurologist and he told me to go to the emergency room. Then they could transfer me to one of the hospitals he was affiliated with later, if needed. They admitted me to the hospital overnight, and then transferred me in the morning to one of his suburban hospitals. Problem was they didn't give me any medications during the evening or night.

This happened on Friday of Memorial Day weekend. In the hospital bed, I was surprised that I had difficulty turning and sitting up on my own. The nurses' aides had to give me complete bed baths and diaper changes. A headache started that got progressively worse each day, that made me dizzy and nauseated anytime I moved my eyes —to try to read or write, even to look down at my lunch plate, then up to the TV screen. It felt like both of my eyes kept sliding to the left. After that I ate with my eyes closed and I stopped watching TV. It was hard to focus. It was difficult to dial phone numbers while shifting from the blurred words in my pocket telephone book, and then back to the phone. Eventually I remembered that I could just ask the operator to dial the number for me.

The nurse called my neurologist. He arrived wearing a Hawaiian floral shirt and shorts. I told him about the bad headache and problems with my vision. He gently said, "I will order an MRI. Sorry this is happening, to be honest I was expecting you to be bedridden by now."

He came again early the next morning and told me, "You've had a small stroke. An occipital stroke. I'm shocked myself." He did another neurological exam on me, then said, "I will order an MRA of your carotid arteries. It is similar to an MRI but uses different software. I will start you on Plavix or Lipitor."

I asked him, "When did I have the stroke?"

"I don't know, maybe Tuesday."

He started me on physical therapy, there Diana stood me in between the parallel bars, but it felt like my feet were stuck to the floor! My feet were close together and not moving. This was the first time since my diagnosis in 2003, that I was unable to stand up or control my legs. She was holding me up with the gait waist belt. This really scared me.

She taught me how to sit up and lie down since my back and arms were weak.

She said, It doesn't look like your eyes are moving back-and-forth, just closed. You should open your eyes while reading, writing, looking down and turning your head. In time your eyes will accommodate.

I reluctantly replied, "Even maintaining eye contact with conversations makes me feel nauseated."

She would purposely talk to me squatting down to my level, or on whichever side bothered me at the time, all while encouraging me to keep my eyes open.

Each day in the hospital, my writing was improving, especially with my left hand. But I'm right-handed and because it was faster, I would try using my right hand but it made me dizzy and sick with a headache. I told my neurologist. He explained, "You had a right-sided stroke. With your eyes, it is not just your left eye. They keep writing 'left eye' in your chart. But is the left side of your left eye, and the left side of the right eye. Remember when you were in grade school, and you used a piece of cardboard while reading so that you only saw one line at a time? That may help you now."

Then he went on and on about Monet and Van Gogh and their visual difficulties. I wanted to scream. I don't want to do abstract painting! I'm not ready for that. Was he trying to quell my enthusiasm? He did not believe I will recover my eyesight or adapt? Aren't I standing after not being able to stand last week?

I told him, "I feel grateful that my condition was not worse."

"He said, "Like a glass half full."

I said, "No. Glad that something better may come of this."

He asked, "Are you able to transfer yourself from the wheelchair to the the bed, and toilet and back again?"

I said, "Yes, I am doing that mostly by myself. But they don't want me to do it alone yet."

He said, "Well, you should be able to go home in a couple of days."

I said, "The physical therapists were talking about me having acute care rehab."

He replied, "I have to look at your chart. It would be good if they can get you walking. But if they only get you transferring, at least you're no worse than when you came here."

I knew I needed to do more than be able to only transfer. I needed to get back to standing and walking at least a short distance, like I was doing before I came to the hospital. I felt like crying but waited until he left.

Intensive Rehabilitation

My neurologist signed me up for intensive physical and occupational therapy. They also did a speech therapy assessment. Respiratory therapy monitored my breathing and bipap machine throughout the night because they said my breathing was too shallow. The transfer papers from the emergency room had a diagnosis of 'generalized weakness with respiratory distress and diminished breath sounds.'

A few nights later, I was lying in a hospital bed, most of my body hurt. Muscle soreness after exercise is to be expected but, in addition I had burning pain from my hips down to my toes, and from my shoulders to my fingertips. I remembered previously feeling like my whole body was on fire daily. Any part of my body that I used burned. When I lived at my aunt's house, I started using my wheelchair more often, and taking the baclofen for muscle spasms, most of the burning pain went away. Now the burning pain is back.

The good news is, the physical therapist told me, "I believe that you won't be needing the wheelchair. You should be able to walk. We can teach you how to walk properly."

She guided my legs, especially my hips. This was exciting news.

Occupational therapist had me opening and closing buttons and snaps. My hands would stop working about halfway through these exercises. She said my fine motor skills were okay. She made the task harder as she gave me instructions to remember to not look down while I was trying to concentrate on tasks with my hands. I felt frustrated and wanted to quit. My challenge is writing and reading. Most of my clothes don't have buttons.

They reported I was progressing well in physical therapy. Early one morning a different occupational therapist came and surprised me with a walker. I used it to walk to the toilet and back to my bed. He also helped me pull my shorts and paper panties up, which felt weird. Although I needed the practice, I would have rather had a female. The walker did help me stand longer. My knees were still bent, and I struggled to keep my balance. Later at 11:30 AM, in the gym the physical therapist also had me walking with the walker.

Preparing to go home, the physical therapist asked me, "Is there anything else I could help you with?"

I told her, "Walking without a walker would be nice, because a walker would get in the way in my small kitchen, also holding onto the walker hurts my hands. She had me walk around the hemibar holding on with only one hand. I did better once I learned the foot pattern, and she showed me how to lead with the right hand. I asked her, "What do I do when I start with the right foot."

She said "It stands on its own. I would be more worried about you using a cane and especially without anything because your left foot drags and you may trip. May need AFO braces."

She walked and walked me, around the parallel bars, to the car and back in the morning. The afternoon, she had me walk to the mat, then the long way from the mat table to the door, into the hallway so I can get the feel of walking on carpet and then finally walked me back to my chair. I felt like I was going to faint, flushed with the sweater I had on, but had no way to take it off while I was holding onto the walker. I no longer felt my legs. I stopped to rest saying that I needed to get my legs, left arm, and my head back. I tried walking some more, but there wasn't much improvement. She offered me my wheelchair, instead I refused it as I slowly walked to my wheelchair chair. Why the heroics on my part, the determination to finish like the requirement to finish everything on my plate?

The good news, which is what gave me the energy to overdo the walking in physical therapy and occupational therapy is that the social worker called to make arrangements for me to go home next week. I wanted to show that I'm really ready to go home!

It will go down in my medical record how many yards I walked in physical therapy, but I will decline all that extra walking from here on out. By pushing my limits, am I given the wrong impression as to how patients with MS or similar symptoms are to be rehabbed? Some doctors advise that those with MS pace themselves so that they don't get overheated which causes the muscles to have temporary paralysis or weakness. There were only minimal variations in the exercise routines of all of us patients in the gym, although most of the other patients had strokes. One of the physical therapy students, said to me while very close to my face, "It will only make you stronger."

Is not quality as important, if not more important, than quantity? That morning, the male physical therapist student commented on how I don't pick up my feet when I'm tired. Later I told the female student that I did the twenty repetitions today without resting in between, so that they could all see what happens to my legs when I do too many repetitions. I also couldn't even feel my legs. None of this was written in my chart, instead only what exercises were done. At least some of the pain was mentioned. However, my decrease in walking distance wasn't from the pain. Didn't they hear or understand anything I said?

The Psychologist

Dr. Zogota, knocked on my door at lunchtime. It was strange to me to have a psychotherapist come to my room. I usually go to their office. I guess it's similar to doctors coming in. He came in and sat in the reclining chair. His hair was shoulder length. He said, "The nurse said you wanted to talk to me."

I said, "I don't know if she told you the reason I want to talk to you. I haven't been able to talk to anyone about the progressive nature of the disease I've been diagnosed with. My sister is in denial, as she is with most serious topics. I did try to talk to my brother too, about my Living Will when I was having problems breathing. My neurologist told me soon after I came into the hospital, that he expected my condition to have declined by now to being bedridden, not be able to walk, talk, feed myself, do anything. It's only been three years since he diagnosed me with spinocerebellar degeneration. I've been doing well for three years, but now this happened. He initially told me it would be a "graduate decline." I live alone and haven't had any noticeable decline of the use of my arms and legs, may have even done better this past year. Now this! May be time to talk about it."

Dr. Zogota let me talk and talk, only saying at the beginning, "You can eat your lunch." But I knew I couldn't talk and eat at the same time. For safety, since I choke easily, as well as conscious of time and memory lapses, I said, "I'll wait. It's a cold plate anyway. Chicken salad, red grapes, and strawberries. Oh, except for a small bowl of rice and a small bowl of canned green beans."

I began by saying, "I didn't let myself think or feel about what is happening to me since I've been in the hospital. At first, I was shocked, everything seemed surreal. But last week, I started to get some clarity. I was able to write more in my journal without getting the terrible headache, nausea, and my writing started to flow."

"How are you able to write better? Was it emotionally, physically or your thinking?"

I stuttered, beginning then pausing, "Yes, physically because I would feel very sick, dizzy and nauseous when I tried to write. Journaling, although difficult, helped me emotionally to open up. I felt a little better here when you asked me about my occupations and hobbies, but it also made me feel sad because I couldn't do them anymore. My thinking improved too because I was better able to finish my sentences and thoughts."

I tried to look at my journal for excerpts to read to him the differences in my clarity, but had difficulty finding the pages.

He surprised me by commenting, "You only wrote a page and a half."

I thought 'How did he know that? Then I realized that he was watching as I turned the pages. Some days I only wrote one or two sentences.

"Yes, in the beginning most of the time I couldn't finish sentences."

I decided to stop looking for the specific pages, and just tell him what I wanted to talk to him about. He listened in silence as I told him what I had told the nurse, adding more to explain.

Last week, he ended his initial routine new patient assessment visit by saying, "I'd like to come back and talk to you some more. I'd like to talk about some of your irritation with staff."

I was comforted and relieved that he understood how annoying it was for staff to repeatedly ask me the same questions over and over. It didn't matter — the regular daily staff plus all the new students, doctors and rehab therapists. Although they were all trained to ask me, 'Do you need anything,' it didn't seem like they were understanding me when I tried to explain how too much physical therapy exercises gave me more spasms and pain.

He had also told me last week, "You are difficult to read because of your smile."

To me he is even harder to read because he kept a straight face. Today, waiting for his response, I went on and ate my lunch, not wanting my rice and green beans to get colder, I asked him, "Aren't you going to say anything?" I was actually worried that he wouldn't say much. But he said a lot.

"You seem calm as you tell me all this."

"I was surprised myself at how peaceful and calm I've been this week. Considering what I went through over the past three weeks."

"I get the feeling that you've been through worse things in your life than having a neuromuscular disease like MS."

"Well, I wondered this morning why I felt so calm. I was thinking maybe it is because I've been through dealing with this already when I started going to my therapist in 2004 to deal with losses. In 1999, I lost my physical health, income, status in a community, career, family and friends. I was homeless. But there are other kinds of losses. I used to belong to an online MS support group where members talked about losing function, grieving then adapting only to have yet another loss, grieving then struggling to adapt some more. This has gone on and on and on, where I barely do much of what I used to do, so that I don't know who I am anymore. Like I don't feel I have an identity. Some religious spiritual beliefs promote giving up one's identity. But it's an awful feeling. In therapy over the past year, I felt fuller, like the void had been filling up. I've done much more in life than I told you, traveled and more. I've wondered if I never do anything else, would I be okay?"

"Has anyone on your health care team told you, you could die in a year? I thought people with MS . . ."

"No. People with MS have almost the same life expectancy as the general population. But there are different types of MS. Some people with MS you wouldn't even know they have it. Others that can be in wheelchairs or bedridden, is rarer. My neurologist told me that even experienced neurologists would only see one or two cases of primary progressive MS throughout their whole career. Primary progressive MS is what he initially diagnosed me with. I have a young friend in her 20's who was bedridden in five years and can't communicate. She could live another 40 to 50 years. I don't want to do that to my family."

Dr. Zogota was silent, but his shift in his seat showed his discomfort and perhaps agreement with me. "You have a very complex personality."

I laughed and said, "Why? You won't find me in a textbook?"

"I won't find any pathology."

"I would be curious what psychology tests would show now. I took some tests in 1990."

"What did the test show?"

"Well, three things. (Blushing). I only remember one."

"What was that one?"

"Delusions of grandeur." (I didn't tell him that the reason why I only remember delusions of grandeur is because it was a Black woman psychologist who did the testing. She didn't consider it pathological, because most Black patients had a higher score for delusions of grandeur on the MMPI Personality assessment. I, of course, didn't know the MMPI back then or what it was for. It is probably because we have to survive, in spite of so much discrimination, oppression, having to overcompensate and succeed with anything that we do. Not bragging, just a normal way of life for us).

"There must've been a lot going well in your life then."

"No, things are not going well at all. I wish I had the test results for comparison to, if

I took the test now. The results would be like night and day. I went away to college and traveled. I've grown even more since I've been using a wheelchair. I've had to learn to speak up, to advocate, blossom and become more sociable.

"What did you do before? You're kind of young to be here."

"I was a nurse, an artist." I didn't tell them the many other things I've done in my life.

"You're a unique person. Most patients give up. They don't have the intelligence, goals, or the creativity that you have. I don't know what to tell you. I can't sugarcoat it. I think you will do fine as long as you don't put off putting your affairs in order."

Previously, I expressed frustration with financial challenges to getting appropriate adaptive equipment that would help me be more independent. The state wouldn't pay for the equipment unless I was going to work. So I was trying to save up to purchase it myself. But I had to move twice last year. I did buy a computer, so that I could use Dragon Naturally Speaking voice recognition dictation voice-to-text computer software, to type for me. Dr. Zogota chatted a little about the Dragon Naturally Speaking, and I gave him some advice for using it himself to help with all the paperwork and charting he has to do.

He wished me well and said, "I'll be looking for your book."

Results

I stayed five weeks total in the hospital. Mother Dear flew in to visit me. My cousin came several times since she lived nearby. Staying extra weeks in the rehabilitation hospital had me worried about my apartment. I gave my cousin my keys to my apartment, to bring my checkbook so I could pay rent because I remember back in 1999, when I was in the hospital followed by a recovery residence, I was told that I would lose my transitional housing with the homeless agency if I stayed away longer than thirty days. Amazingly and gratefully when I called and talked to my current apartment manager, she assured me that, "Don't worry about paying your rent while you are there. Just get well. This is your home now."

A month after coming home, I read about the MS hug. An MS hug is often the beginning of an MS exacerbation.

The tight sensation around my ribs that wouldn't let me take a deep breath. Then I got weaker, where I had difficulty even sitting up or turning over in bed. Also, what my neurologist initially diagnosed me with — progressive relapsing MS —starts out gradually worsening, but later has acute attacks. But when I showed him this information, he argued that all neurological diseases have relapses whenever they have an infection. He did consider giving me IV steroids while I was in the hospital but changed his mind.

I think it is also possible that I may have had a TIA (transient ischemic attack) temporary brief mini stroke, although the neurologist told me that he had mistakenly thought another patient's MRI was mine, and therefore I didn't have a stroke. What if it was actually my MRI pictures, but I had recovered from the stroke before follow-up MRI's were done?

Chapter 6: Another Before My Time

In 2003, soon after I was diagnosed with brucellosis, there was an article in a nursing magazine about Florence Nightingale suffering from depression and went on and on about her having depression, even Bipolar Disorder. Florence Nightingale also had brucellosis. Crimean fever is what brucellosis was called back in the 1800's. She probably acquired brucellosis in ways similar to how I did from milking an unvaccinated cow and eating unpasteurized milk in the form of yogurt while I was Zimbabwe. In addition, I helped hold a baby goat for an injection. Assumptions were made in the article as to psychological reasons why she took to her bed, even after almost dying of the high fevers. Her being in a war, nursing wounded soldiers, along with speculating that she was grieving because her mother died could be traumatizing and depressing.

More recent articles defended her symptoms as being physical not psychological. Back in the 1800s doctors diagnosed her with neurasthenia psychosomatic or hysteria. One doctor said she was lazy and didn't want to work! How could a doctor say she had mental illness when she didn't really ever stop working in spite of the awful pain that I know all too well. Brucellosis is very difficult to diagnose in humans. It can affect the nervous system, joints, heart, and digestive system. Symptoms come and go, so that is why she was able to still be productive. However, because she was productive, described with "superhuman effort" often pushing herself to work 20 hours a day when she could, the other days she would be very sick, therefore, a doctor decided that she had bipolar! He assumed these were manic episodes.

Florence Nightingale was unable to walk for six years, and although she was mostly bedridden this is when she did the most writing and correspondence with officials to establish nursing as a profession starting when she was only in her 30s. She promoted supportive services and employment for other nurses. Since she was good in mathematics and statistics, she was able to include diagrams and research in her manuals. Florence Nightingale founded the first nursing textbook, the first nursing training school, and the field of public health. She lived to be 90 years old.

Same with me, when I had chest pains and was beginning to have difficulty walking, not admitting they did not know what was wrong with me, the doctors sent me to a psychiatrist.
It wasn't until four years later, after three previous neurologists, that a new neurologist that the infectious disease doctor referred me to, did more MRI's and added the diagnosis of spinocerebellar degeneration.

Florence Nightingale wasn't the only one experiencing war traumas or Brucellosis. Why me out of my half a dozen siblings, was I the only one in my family who was diagnosed with spinocerebellar degeneration that is usually a hereditary degenerative neuromuscular disease. And of my classmates, the only one who came back with brucellosis? I'm was probably more cautious with food, activities, and hand washing than they were!

Florence Nightingale was given credit for revolutionizing hospital care by promoting the necessity of fresh air, good food, and clean water for drinking and sanitation and personal hygiene that decreased infections and therefore unnecessary deaths of soldiers. Often having to sneak in to care for the soldiers at night after the male officer doctors would go to bed. Doctors back then didn't want women nurses.

Well, in the process of doing recent online research, looking for Florence

CHAPTER 6: ANOTHER BEFORE MY TIME   79

Nightingale's birthdate to see what personality traits we have in common, I was stopped in my tracks by a photo of an African American woman, Mary Jane Grant Seacole, who also did nursing. Born fifteen years earlier than Florence Nightingale, she actually did much more than nursing. Mary Seacole was a doctoress, herbalist and businesswoman from Jamaica who had experience saving many lives from tropical diseases, even worked alongside military doctors before the Crimean War, yet was denied by the British War Office to serve as a nurse because she was Black. Florence Nightingale also would not allow Mary Seacole to join her nurses although Mary Seacole was light complexion being of mixed heritage. They did talk and sometimes met together, therefore it is possible that Mary Seacole taught

Florence Nightingale about hygiene and sanitation that she had already been using for years prior. Mary Seacole's personal history and contributions to the world are fascinating. Her accomplishments are astounding for any person, especially women, then and now. She wrote her own autobiography, <u>Wonderful Adventures of Miss Seacole in Many Lands</u> (1857) and she traveled independently with her own money, that she made herself as a doctor and business woman, providing many different services. She owned hotels and stores. Her story goes on and on in Wikipedia for each decade of her life. Mary Seacole was fearless. A true heroine on and off the battlefield.

I also tend to be fearless, although I do less traveling now when using a wheelchair. Whatever needs to be done, wherever I am divinely guided to go, I go.

PART TWO: LIFE USING A WHEELCHAIR

Chapter 7: Getting a Wheelchair

Emotionally it was difficult to think of what it was like to go from walking miles to being totally exhausted after walking two blocks. Other than taking a bus for long distances, I previously walked almost everywhere because I never had a car. In Zimbabwe I walked two hours over rough terrain up and down hills to and two hours back from villages. Approximately six months after I returned to the United States I began having difficulty walking up the huge mound in the middle of the streets. You are probably thinking, "Huh, what mounds? Well, I too never noticed the gradual incline and declines on either side of the streets where cars are usually parked before neither. A taxi driver observing me one day said, "You look like you are trying to climb a mountain. Soon after, climbing stairs became almost impossible and then impossible.

Used to doing at least twenty activities a day, I learned to be grateful for accomplishing only one or two tasks a day. This was very humbling, but also terrifying for me to have to depend on other people for my physical needs. My legs would collapse with little warning. With reluctance, after reading an article about a doctor with multiple sclerosis who gave in and started to use a wheelchair saw it actually gave him more freedom and ability to do more activities because he had less fatigue. I too, discovered with using an electric power wheelchair I had less pain and exhaustion. Gave me my independence back.

My first wheelchair, a Golden Alante was delivered within two weeks, ten days before Christmas in 2001. The wheelchair technician had me practice driving it in the apartment building's wide hallway. He told me not to worry about accidentally scraping the walls because the landlord couldn't sue me for it. Then he left. Left me in the doorway of my small efficiency studio apartment to figure out how to get the wheelchair all the way inside without breaking my furniture or me. Frustrated, I cried. He hadn't shown me how to turn, go sideways or backwards. Being me, I kept at it until I parked it with minimal damage. Taught myself how to drive the wheelchair from then on out.

The most useful information the wheelchair technician told me was to let my wheelchair push open doors for me instead of with my arms. I didn't remember the reason why, because he told me a lot that day. I wish I had heeded his warning because over time I badly injured my left shoulder. Our arms aren't really designed to repeatedly be in a backwards position as we hold the door open long enough to drive the wheelchair forward. Now, I ask for help. It's weird though, I knock on doors, and from across the room I hear, "It's open."

I knock again.

"It's open!"

They come to the door, don't see me and walk away. Or puzzled say, "The door is not locked." Or opened gratefully with a smile, "Oh, come on in."

Insurances didn't give us a choice in wheelchairs. A wheelchair technician from a medical supply company came out to your home, measured your height, width and depth, and noted whether you are right-handed, left-handed, or no-handed. Maybe they ask you what color you prefer. Then he returned in a couple of months with a wheelchair. I wish it was like going to a car dealership where we could test drive a variety of brands and styles. Some wheelchairs have front wheel drive meaning the largest wheel is in the front. Rear wheel drive is when the largest wheel is in the back. Whether a wheelchair is a front wheel or rear wheel drive, believe me this makes a huge difference in steering a wheelchair. When I received my Permobil in 2003, it had rear wheel drive, it was like learning how to maneuver a wheelchair for the first time.

Usually insurances will only pay for a new wheelchair after you had it for five years. Heaven blessed me otherwise. I went to the Abilities Expo where they have educational workshops, entertainment, and vendors selling different types of wheelchairs, equipment, accessible vans, and assistive technology. This is where I learned about Dragon Naturally Speaking software that allows you to talk and it types for you. What drew my attention though, was a a beautiful blue bathtub apparatus that would lower me down into the tub and when finished bathing, rises to the top of the bathtub and sits me up. The last time I'd been in a bathtub was in 2001 when my legs suddenly wouldn't move. I didn't know then that any time my body was overheated I would get paralyzed. My helper struggled for a long time to try different ways to get me out. She did eventually. But that was too scary to even think about ever trying again.

I scheduled an appointment for the dealer to come out to my home to measure the bathtub and me. He asked me, "What's your diagnosis for why you are using a wheelchair?"

"Multiple sclerosis." (A previous neurologist wrote possible multiple sclerosis on a physical therapy prescription).

"That's the wrong wheelchair for a progressive disease. How long have you had this wheelchair?"

"Two years."

"Well, usually you can only get a new wheelchair after you had it for five years, but they gave you the wrong prescription. With smaller wheelchair companies they are going to give you the cheapest wheelchair because insurances only pay up to $5000. If the wheelchair cost more, then the company takes a loss. In addition, the company basically just gave you a wheelchair out of a box on their shelves. A one size fits most. It didn't even make sense for them to measure you."

He made the arrangements and returned in a few months with a huge Permobil power wheelchair. At least he took plenty time to show me how to drive it, how to go backwards which I simply avoided until then, and how to get out of tight spaces.

"Pull forward as you turn." He repeated this several times until I got it. I've been grateful to him ever since.

Besides my new wheelchair being bigger, and not designed to take apart like the Golden Alanté, it had several advantages. Customized to fit my body, it had a seat cushion, side supports to keep me from leaning or falling forward, leg side supports to prevent my thighs from embarrassingly gaping open, it tilted and reclined to relieve pressure on my butt, decreased backaches, with a shock absorber suspension system underneath for a more comfortable ride. The Permobil wheelchair is a European import, built sturdy like their cars. Unlike my Golden Alanté, that probably was designed for home use only, had multiple major repairs within the first six months of having it: the back of the chair broke, and later both the front motors had to be replaced. It seemed every time I went over just a crack in the sidewalk something broke. Although I was gentle and cautious, same as I am with the rest of my life, it would break. To this day, I still tense up and get an automatic startle reflex whenever I accidentally go over a larger crack in the sidewalk. In contrast, the Permobil wheelchair requires very little maintenance. For the price tag of $18,000 versus $5000 that's how it should be!

Now by law, we are required to get fitted in a hospital physical therapy department by a rehabilitation assistive technology professional or occupational therapist.

Some rehabilitation hospitals do have several different style wheelchairs to test drive along with expert supervision. So far, I've not been that lucky, because of course it's what everyone would prefer so it takes too long to get an appointment. A compromise was having an assistive technology professional from a wheelchair company evaluate me in the presence of a rehabilitation medical doctor. Again, I never saw what my newest wheelchair would be until it was brought to my home.

Chapter 8: Not for the Faint of Heart

The old buses back in the early 2000s, had hydraulic lifts that would break down whenever the weather temperature was too hot or too cold, shutting down the whole hydraulic system, that meant the bus couldn't go anywhere. Therefore, bus drivers regularly passed up people in wheelchairs waiting at the bus stops. The newer buses now have long flip-out ramps that come out after the side of the bus kneels down lower. Because of the ability of the bus to lower still depends on hydraulics, occasionally when it's really hot in the summer the new buses break down too. Twice this happened to me when I was on a 147 express bus when it sputtered and stopped on DuSable Lakeshore Drive. All the other passengers could get off the bus and transfer to other buses that came along, except me because since the whole electrical system was down, the driver couldn't let the ramp out. In addition, there was no sidewalk to put the ramp on. The angle would have been too steep. I had to wait on the bus, with the driver until the supervisor and later the roadside assistance came.

Another time the bus ahead of us on DuSable Lake Shore Drive had a small fire, stopping all southbound shoulder traffic. Fireman came to help get me off the bus. One fireman on either side and another standing in front of me kept me and my wheelchair from tipping forward while going down the steep wheelchair ramp onto the shoulder of Lake Shore Drive. Then the firemen safely guided me onto inner Lake Shore Drive near Belmont Avenue where I could catch a bus to the university downtown.

I'm glad the firemen let me stay in my wheelchair because I don't like to be carried. I was dropped a few times prior to getting a wheelchair. Usually by men who wanted to be heroes and carry me on stairs by themselves. Sweating while carrying me up the stairs, then hours later they tended to struggle as they got tired near the bottom of the stairs, dropping me on my back on the sharp edge of a stair.

My most terrifying incident in my wheelchair was when I had asked the bus driver to get the bus as close to the curb as possible to put the full length of the ramp on the sidewalk. She had a jeering attitude a couple of times before, as if she had a grudge against anyone with a disability. This time I was begging her before she got to the stop, but she didn't. For some reason or another my new wheelchair I received in 2014 tipped dangerously forward on steep declines and the new curb cuts. Sometimes when I took a peek out the bus's door and saw the ramp was going to be too steep when the drivers put it down, I would ride to the next bus stop and hopefully it would be better placed. But I underestimated this time, plus with the driver's attitude there was no guarantee that she would park the bus any better further down the street. So I ventured out the bus door. Teetering in the middle of the ramp, I could go neither backwards into the bus nor go forward, without my wheelchair threatening to dump me face first onto the sidewalk with over 300 pounds of machinery on top of me. The bus driver didn't get out of her seat nor say anything to help. There was a small crowd of people waiting to get on the bus. They just stood there. Most were older people but there was a good looking muscular young man near the front of the crowd. Time stood still, until I gained enough clarity of mind to call out to him. He came over and up the ramp, held onto the front of my wheelchair supporting and guiding it down safely onto the sidewalk. I hugged and thanked him as I sobbed with relief. He gratefully hugged back. And I continued on my way. I was so shook up, I rode myself the rest of the way home rather than get on another bus. I reported the driver to the transit authorities, perhaps those who witnessed the incident did too because now all of the bus drivers pull in close to the curb and let the ramps down fully onto the sidewalks.

Chapter 9: Trains

I had not experienced problems while on the elevated nor subway trains in Chicago until recently. At the Clark and State station, there were sounds of fighting in the subway, yelling, screaming, cursing, glass breaking. The train engineer, who drives the train, told us we will be at a standstill waiting for the police. Meanwhile the power was cut to the train. I guess there was risk of someone being pushed onto the tracks. We had dimmed lights, but it meant the train couldn't go anywhere. He left the doors open allowing more and more people to squeeze into the train. No one seemed to care about COVID and social distancing. They just wanted to get home. Later the engineer told everyone to get off the train and go upstairs to take other transportation but told me to stay. He got off the train a few times to tell the police that gathered on that platform what he had witnessed, which was different from what the woman who was causing the trouble was telling the police. Allegedly, she was randomly spraying people with mace.

Imagine what it was like for everyone to evacuate the train, including the train engineer, and leave you alone on the train in your wheelchair. I couldn't get off the train because the platform was higher than the train doorway. Someone, usually station attendants or the train engineer will bring the yellow gap filler ramp. Luckily, after a half hour, the electrical power was restored, and the train continued in route without further incidents.

The second time this happened, I was on the Orange Line train at Midway Airport station. As the train pulled out it kept starting, stopping, and mildly jerking. The train engineer stopped the train, then walked through the train to the other end and drove the train back into the Midway Airport station. She told everyone to get off the train. They did, but then she closed the train doors and left me. I saw two cleaning staff on the platform, so I knocked on the train door. They were talking to a middle-aged man wearing all navy blue. As he came closer, I saw he had a pin on his sweater similar to airline pilot wings. He was another train engineer. He calmly came over, opened the door, and with the gap filler ramp got me off the train.

He asked me, "Do you want to get on the other train? We are about to depart now."

I nodded and said, "Yes."

It all happened so fast. Somehow, I deep breathed and didn't panic. What could have been a wheelchair user's worst nightmare, didn't sink in until a few days later, as I realized my fellow Americans were in such a hurry that they did not look back to see if I needed help. This scene played over and over in my mind. I decided then that it really wasn't safe for me to take the train anymore for a while. Not until the COVID pandemic, staff, food and housing shortages decrease so that homeless people or not so desperate to have a warm place to stay that they're hoping to be arrested and jailed. They stay in elevators overnight, urinating, sometimes defecating and breaking elevators so people with disabilities can't take the train. My empathy goes out to them, In the meantime, it is best for me to take the paratransit vans, hopefully to get a straight ride to my destination and back home safely.

Chapter 10: Paratransit Services

When there is snow, rain, heat or cold I have to take special paratransit vans or taxicabs that have a ramp and a large space for people in wheelchairs. Paratransit service provides "door-to-door" transportation instead of having to wait on bus stops. Sounds great, but it is "a shared ride." We have to call the day before our trip to schedule a ride for the next day. It's best to call as close to 6:00 AM to get the pickup times you want. Otherwise the reservationists will tell you there are no times available within that hour.

Taxicabs were promoted as allowing us to take spontaneous trips, like anybody else, and be the only passenger in the taxicab, instead of riding in a paratransit van full of other passengers. Initially, we could purchase taxi vouchers for $5 to cover a $13 trip. The catch was that the vouchers expired in six months. While people who walk could get a taxi right away, those of us using wheelchairs couldn't call any of the taxicab companies directly. Instead, we had to call a central citywide phone number and they would send us a taxicab. We didn't get to choose the cab company. They might send us a Yellow, Flash, or Blue Ribbon taxicab. There were fewer wheelchair accessible taxicabs, only fifty for all of Chicago, so it could take an hour or more for the taxicab to come. Sometimes I would go with a friend or helper who could push me in my little transport wheelchair, then a cab would come in five minutes. Occasionally I took a taxi home from the university at night and told the dispatcher I'd pay cash instead of a voucher, and the drivers came right away.

Later, I temporarily stopped using taxis when it took me three hours for a taxicab to come get me from the grocery store. Due to this gross inconvenience, I was losing money since there were no refunds on the taxicab vouchers. I only kept a few vouchers for emergencies. Over the years, there were improvements when more independent taxi companies were added. Fares became $3 for a $15 destination, and we now use a debit type card instead of handwritten paper carbon copy vouchers. During the COVID pandemic fares were free up to $30.

Some good that came out of the COVID pandemic shut down, was initially only one passenger was in the regular Pace minivans. Plus, they started occasionally sending taxis for me at the paratransit price of $3.25. How now I wish that Pace would give me a taxi regularly! After the worst of the two years of COVID pandemic was over, Pace returned to squeezing as many passengers as possible into mid-size buses. It has taken two to three hours to get to doctor appointments, university, work or other activities and longer to arrive home. You could try to plan scheduling a much earlier pickup time and still arrive late.

The main problem is the many add-ons. Some days, the closer I got to my home, the dispatcher adds other passenger pick-ups and drop-offs to the route, making the driver go west and south of my home three times only for the customers to not be there. Drivers have taken me past my apartment building to drop off someone who got into the van after I did. If I'm coming from far south to go far north, the drivers should really be taking the expressways either I-55 or I-94 into DuSable Lake Shore Drive cutting the travel time to an hour, maybe an hour and a half during rush hour. That many passengers shouldn't ever be put on my route home or to work in the morning, especially when they are that far away from my destination.

It is wonderful when Pace surprises me with a taxi ride. the taxi drivers will call and tell me their estimated time of arrival and if they may be late. Even if "late," I don't mind because I know they will still get me there on time. Another benefit, as with other paratransit rides, the varied conversations during long commutes are precious as we learn from each other.

I like my independence and freedom to go and return when I choose. In the spring, I bust loose. Inhaling the smell of flowers and budding trees, wheeling myself along the way. If you are wondering where I escaped to, you'll find me gleefully shopping anywhere or in a city park.

Folks suggest I get my own car or van. Sounds like a good idea to drive myself wherever I need to go. However, price of a wheelchair accessible van starts at $80,000 to $100,000 and that price is for a basic van similar to the paratransit van where someone else chauffeurs me around. A customized modified van with hand controls since our legs wouldn't be able to step on the gas or the brakes, costs more. I'd need special mirrors since I don't have peripheral vision in my left eye. Plus, the cost of special driving lessons may be only partially paid by some insurances for rehabilitation physical therapist specialists. Not to mention having to move to a warmer climate, so as to not have to find somebody to shovel me out from wherever I'm parked!

Chapter 11: By Air

The airport crew broke my wheelchair. This was despite me putting simple instructions in large font on a large card on the back of the wheelchair. I wondered why I was waiting a long time for them to bring my power wheelchair to the plane's door. Waited so long that the plane had to leave. After waiting awhile in the waiting area, down the hallway was coming a man with my wheelchair. The top of the chair was folded in half, kissing the seat. I yelled, "Oh, no!"

CHAPTER 11: BY AIR   113

I was relieved when he opened it up and helped me into my wheelchair. But then he said, "Ma'am, you need to go to the claim's department."

He didn't tell me the United Airlines claim's department was all the way on the other side of O'Hara Airport! Up and down several elevators, through the long hallway and beside the airport pedestrian walkways that are similar to escalators except it moves flat along the floor for over a mile. We were trying to hurry because I had a scheduled paratransit ride home. Down another elevator to the baggage area was the United Airlines claim's department. The clerk explained that United Airlines does not pay for a replacement of wheelchairs, they only will do repairs. They will send a wheelchair repairperson to my home in the next day or two. We made it home, but soon after, the upper part of my wheelchair seat suddenly fell completely backwards! What if that had happened while we were going through the long underground tunnel with no one to ask for help if I were injured?

The wheelchair mechanic came the next day. He put metal rods on each side to hold the back straight up. Luckily, I still had the Golden Alante for an emergency wheelchair. I told him that the batteries were low. He brought and installed two new batteries the next day. This was good however, I still needed my Permobil wheelchair for outside my home. Remember, the Golden Alanté wheelchair tended to break even when going over a small crack in the sidewalk. However the straight up position on the back of my Permobil wheelchair gave me severe backaches. So I prayed often to make it through the day.

Chapter 12: Invisible

A couple of weeks later, I'm at my therapist Monica's office trying to explain my frustration with waiting to get my wheelchair fixed or a new wheelchair, plus the whole messed up air travel experience. How I really needed a personal assistant when I go to conferences, because I could barely move the first two days after I traveled. Packing before I even get there tired me out. Previously, before I became disabled, I would start packing two weeks ahead of time. As I thought of items, I would throw them in an open suitcase. And then followed up with a list I checked off. For years, I was not a last minute person. The past two times I traveled, I packed a couple of days before. And then I forgot to bring some important medical equipment and had to suffer the consequences. Most people didn't know how much I had to push myself up and beyond both my physical and emotional capabilities the whole time that I was away at the conference.

Monica asked, "Are there organizations for professional people with disabilities? Where you won't feel so lonely? Who have to struggle the way you do? Who may have tips for traveling?"

Well, there is the Progress Center for Independent Living where most of the staff has a disability. I really wanted to say, 'Sure I know a lot of people with disabilities, who hardly go anywhere because their homes have stairs, they were not given adequate electric wheelchairs and the constant challenges are too difficult. Emotionally, it gets tempting to give up. Therefore when I do go out, I feel lonely. There are two extremes: either young men who use the small racer type wheelchairs who can drive their own cars, and then there are people who have to depend on someone to do almost everything for them.

Even at the conference for rehabilitation psychologists, the psychologists with disabilities were ignored at a social event that was scheduled in the hotel's restaurant bar. The waitress told me, "The ramp has been broken since November. This is February. They put out extra tables in the hallway for you who use wheelchairs."

She led me to the empty tables and asked, "Would you like to order a drink or food?"

I responded, "Not now. Putting extra tables here does not solve the problem. This is supposed to be a social! Why are they over there, and I am stuck out here?"

It was then that I noticed another young woman sitting on her scooter at a table with a young man. I don't know how long she been sitting there. It was 9 PM, the social was supposed to have started at 7 PM. I'd been talking to someone else about a technology games exhibit and lost track of time. Caroline introduced herself and her husband to me. And said, "Yes, this is the women's rehabilitation psychology group and we've wondered why they didn't come down here to join me. It is as if I am invisible."

Monica said, "You all didn't ask them to come down?"

I said, "Why should we? They're supposed to be rehabilitation psychologists. Caroline probably didn't ask them because earlier the wheelchair transportation company didn't come to get her from the airport. They had to call a colleague to come and get them with a regular vehicle which meant having to take her scooter apart and putting it back together again. So she arrived to the conference late. She was probably too tired to fight yet another battle. And why should we be the ones to always go the extra mile?"

I did network with other people with disabilities there, and they are all working professionals. But I was the only African American using a wheelchair. Previously a mentor advised me that I would have to go up to people and network. And I did, I'm not shy, I reached out each day I was at the conference. It didn't help that the reception area was so small I could barely move anywhere in the room in my wheelchair. And what do you do when you're the only dark complexion person in conference rooms of 200 people? Again, why should I have to be the one to always have to go the extra mile?

Chapter 13: Wheelchair Coming On!

"Wheelchair coming on!" The driver yells to other passengers on the bus.

Paratransit van drivers regularly say, "I have to go and pick up another wheelchair."

Rarely would they ever have to go to an address to just bring out a wheelchair. I've tried gently correcting the drivers by saying, "Oh, you are going to go get someone else who uses a wheelchair. What is their name?"

They may respond with the name of a person as if I know them. Point well taken. May even apologize. However, most of the time this goes right over the driver's head. It is difficult to repeatedly hear that instead of looking forward to welcoming another customer, some drivers and dispatchers refer to us as an object or worse an inconvenience.

The Art Institute of Chicago hosted the Bisa Butler quilt exhibit during the summer of 2021. Two older black women standing ahead of us were talking about quilting. I asked them, "Are there Black quilter groups in Chicago? Where?"

Turning to my friend, instead of me she said, "There is one on the Southside. You can look it up online for her. Just go to the park district website."

As I started to show her, on my cellphone the pictures of quilts I made, she turned and walked away.

This slight was forgiven soon after, as a middle-aged Black security guard saw we were looking at an old black and white photo next to a quilt. He came over next to me, smiling, looking at me directly and excitedly told me, "A young woman came in and told me that that was an old picture of her mother, that Bisa Butler used the photo to design the large colorful quilt next to it!"

He acknowledged me as a person and an elder with grey hair. I returned the favor by excited telling him, "You witnessed and are yourself now a part of history as your picture was taken with the artist Bisa Butler and the now famous daughter!"

In my own family recently one of my brothers told me, "I didn't come visit you before because you were boring."

Huh? What did he mean? I am the same me. The only difference is now I have more confidence and do walk more around my apartment. I have always done creative projects, cooked, went out, worked and traveled. Then I remembered, perhaps is because he and my other siblings and cousins went out to clubs, casinos etc. without even inviting me. They always assumed that I would stay home with my grandmother. To me going out to clubs is boring. And how most of my family sits around and watches TV when visiting or they're not at work is boring too.

Chapter 14: University

No Seat at the Table

The ethics class teacher announced that we were moving to a larger classroom. The other students didn't know I emailed the teacher with the request, "Could the extra chairs and tables be moved out of the entrance to our classroom by Thursday?" I ccd the person in charge of ADA accessibility in the student service department, and also the program deans just in case our classroom teacher was not on campus the days before class.

For months, the extra tables from the university group activity room were lining the walls of the hallways. Bravely, I navigated through this obstacle challenge plus the students passing through or socializing sitting on or standing by the tables. But now the overflow of tables were pushed into adjacent classrooms.

Later, the teacher emailed me that she was not authorized to move the furniture. She also sent an email to the deans and student services department, who assigned us classroom 1311A. Our ethics teacher sent us students an email the morning of our class.

I arrived ten minutes early to get a "good seat" I parked my wheelchair at a table "desk" but then I saw there were only 11 chairs, with possibly space for 12 students. We would have 15 students if everyone came. I moved my wheelchair to the outside corner of the tables to allow for one more chair. My large Permobil motorized wheelchair can't fit under most tables anyway.

The teacher came in and quietly asked me, "Do you have enough table space."

Not wanting to draw any more attention, I replied, I'm okay but there are only 12 seats."

She spilled her coffee as she tried to squeeze past my wheelchair. She exclaimed, "This room is not any bigger than the other one! I'm going to find another classroom," as she left.

She returned quickly and said, "We are moving to room 1311D." All my classmates got up and went out of the classroom except for the teacher and myself, as we waited for a student dropping things as she tried to quickly gather her belongings. "Sorry," she said, "I'm trying to get out of your way so you can get past."

I said, "You're okay. Take your time. It's more important to be safe."

As I was the last person out of the room, no one thought to save a space for me. The student who fumbled with her belongings arrived at the first available chair at the same time as I did. She again thought of me and moved to another seat. The teacher got to observe all of this.

I sent her an email thanking the teacher for the room change, explaining that I usually get to class early in order to push the furniture out of the way so my wheelchair will fit. In the other classroom there was no space for me to push the extra chairs out of the way or move the tables further in so my wheelchair would fit, and students could get past. The teacher could see for herself why I needed to be the first person into the classroom not the last. Perhaps it is because when empty, the new classroom looked deceptively larger. But here again, were extra chairs stacked up behind me in the walkway, making it frustrating, to try to back up to position my wheelchair as it frequently bumped into the chairs. For four years, I've become accustomed to arriving early to classrooms to push the tables towards the center of the room to widen the walkway. Otherwise students rushing out at break time and at the end of class don't think to push their chairs in, and this made it difficult for me to get in, if I arrived on time or late. When students are already in their seats, I then have backpacks, purses, and coats on the floor to contend with.

Way back when I was in elementary school, the teachers would tell little children "Stand up and push your chairs in" before they dismissed the class. Perhaps they thought of liabilities and got tired of kissing foreheads, knees, and telephones when they had to report injuries to the principal and the parents. Ironically, since this was an ethics class, we were studying laws to protect the rights of clients, and to do no harm. What about us graduate students? Does the university care about us or the faculty? How can we even care about clients, when we have become so selfish just to get grades, and survive somehow in the rest of our lives? With our actions on automatic pilot how can we think ethically about other people? We forget about other people because we're forced to forget about our Self.

On my way home, I thought of my role in this situation. In an effort to not draw attention to myself in classrooms among my peers and teachers, I may have spoiled everyone by trying to do the problem-solving all by myself. Could I have yelled, "Save a seat for me" as my classmates rushed in the room?" Did I appear to be passive? Have I become too passive as I sit by waiting? I don't even go out at break time because I have to push all the chairs in to get past them. In addition, it would take me longer to get down the elevator and return in time. Not to mention having to get past people's chairs again if I'm late. Last semester, teachers and students did ask me if I wanted anything, before they went downstairs. One teacher even offered to pay for a snack or drink. But I have a gluten-free diet. Most food items in the vending machines or food court are sandwiches or pasta. Drinks would be okay, but I couldn't tell them, although I wore a diaper with extra pads I don't want to wet my pants all the way home as the Chicago potholes in the streets make the van ride shake all the pee out of me!

If I continue to move the furniture myself, and tell people "No thank you" when they offer to help, they'll think I don't need any help. But how to get a balance between not wanting people to assume I'm helpless and therefore a burden, and my over proving that I'm independent enough? My sore shoulder won't allow me to keep yanking doors open and pulling chairs out of the way. My new wheelchair doesn't seem to be as strong as my old wheelchair was for pushing heavy furniture like the classroom tables out of the way. Now I have to be concerned about protecting my new wheelchair. The economy has affected us all, as insurances are reluctant to pay for repairs and companies have downsized, or gone out of business all together. Understaffed, the wheelchair company had me wait weeks for even major repairs. Previously they came the same day or the next day or at least the same week.

Similarly, the university downsized their employees. There used to be an employee who made sure the classroom furniture and supplies were set up early each morning. There were written notices in each classroom to not move furniture into other classrooms. When I thanked my teacher for moving the class to a larger room, I added the simple statement that there used to be an employee to move the furniture. I was trying to be tactful, and gently pointing out that moving us to a larger room will not solve the wheelchair accessibility problem, because anyone could dump extra furniture in the new classroom too at any time.

By ethical standards, psychologist cannot discriminate by denying therapy to clients with disabilities simply because their offices are not accessible. The teacher did ask me loudly, "Haneefa, do you have enough space at the table?" In other classrooms, she asked me, "Haneefa, you have anything to write on" since I would use my lap to write on when there was no room at the tables for me at all. Perhaps that was her way of drawing my peers' attention to the situation that I needed to be included. These are "teachable moment," but is it my responsibility to always teach? And to always problem solve? Classroom teachers could be the role model as to what to do in these situations. We are all learning.

In the crowded classroom, a student had us move out-of-the-way while she moved another table into place so there would be enough seats. But still there was not enough room for me. If I had been standing or sat on the floor people probably would have been uncomfortable and said, "No, we will move over so we can all sit down and fit at the tables. Years ago, beginning when I was a teenager, family and other people always protested, "Why don't you have a seat," when I was the only one standing. I often stood because sitting in chairs caused me excruciating back pain. Now in classrooms it may be possible if I lower my new wheelchair to fit under the desk but when my wheelchair is not tilted upwards and back, I get backaches.

Spiritually, I wondered what to do to improve my situation and have places accessible for me and others who use wheelchairs. What does it mean to not have a place at the table?" Even when I do have a seat at the table I'm still set apart because I can't break bread together. Aware that my wheelchair sets me apart in my home too, I now sit on the futon couch with my guest for at least a little while. But there is no space for a table in my home.

With Fen Sui, red-colored accents along with loveseats or pairs of chairs are recommended to attract guests and mates to a home. The few chair seats that I do have, and every other surface is full already! Mostly full of textbooks and papers. Since reading about Fen Sui, I've made more of an effort to make space before anyone comes, and to keep the recliner in my bedroom and the spare wheelchair in the living room clear at all times. But when it really comes down to the underlying feeling and reality, there's no space in my apartment for anyone to feel welcome! Not even myself! Although friends have tried to help organize and rearrange it as they are usually used to doing, they don't understand that most homes are traditionally arranged for people who only sit around watching television or playing video games. I have to squeeze in storage of my textbooks and craft supplies while still having room to maneuver my wheelchair.

Meanwhile, symbolically, there's no room in my life for me neither, as the graduate school doctoral program demanded all of my thinking space twenty-four/seven. This year, I admit I don't have energy and patience to extend my remaining reserve to family and friends. And I'm sure they could feel that although I was physically present, my mind was far away analyzing and planning for the next deadline. Much as I wanted to be with my grandmother in Philadelphia there was no space for her or I at her apartment. Family members forget, same as at the university that I do need help, because I tend to push myself to be as independent as possible. This can be physically exhausting.

Chapter 15: University: Tarot Card Guidance

The Church of the Spirit had a summer workshop series on recognizing and working with spirit in daily life. There was a workshop, "Tarot as a Tool for Spiritual Unfoldment." I previously avoided tarot because I assumed tarot cards were used for fortune telling by psychics. Plus, the amount of cards in a deck seemed complicated and scary to me. It was suggested we bring a deck of Rider-Wait cards with us to the workshop.

Dr. Kenneth James, a medium and Jungian analyst psychologist led the workshop and explained that although Spiritualists are advised to seek direct communication through a medium or personally, tarot cards can be used to enhance our connections to spirit. Using one's own intuition is best, while getting a feel for the card in your hand and the immediate message while looking at the colors and symbols on the card. He discouraged the use of tarot books for interpretation, except for perhaps one book, <u>Holistic Tarot: An Integrative Approach to Using Tarot for Personal Growth</u>. He gave a quick overview of basic meanings of the minor and major arcana as well as the suits of cups, wands, swords and pentacles. Then instructed us to silently ask a question of spirit, then to pull from our own deck three cards, and lay them out on the table in front of each of us.

CHAPTER 15: UNIVERSITY: TAROT CARD GUIDANCE 143

Love? That's the question that came to my mind. Most of the time I don't think about love or seeking a relationship. Curious and amused, I followed Dr. James' instructions. I turned over the Overview (right side card) IX Swords, Challenge (middle card) IX Hermit, and then last the Action (left side card, reversed) IV Emperor. When I saw the Hermit card, I put my head down and sobbed a little. It's difficult to have a close relationship with people, alone up on top of a mountains by yourself. The same characteristics as a Saturday born person, a loner. The pictures on the other cards also described me very well, including my overall and current challenges. At home, I read the interpretations:

Overview: IX Swords. Lots of feelings of loss. Picture of a woman sitting, in a dark room on a bed, looking depressed. May tend to blame myself for what happened by thinking I could have prevented it. However, what happened was unavoidable and not in my control for reasons I don't understand now. True, sometimes I have a surreal feeling of being unsure of what is real or not. I have had a lot of losses of family and friends that had me feeling I could have done more, and now has me hesitant to get really close to new people.

Challenge: IX Hermit. The Hermit represents wisdom, guidance, and mentoring. I need to be open to advice from those who are wiser than me. Tend to be nonviolence, compassionate, and have gift of prophesy. Hermits take a solitary path to acquire wisdom. That's nice, I like doing artistic crafts and reading but too many solitary activities can be lonely as I tend to frequently leave other people out.

Action: IV Emperor. Represents authorities, dominance, superiority, fire yang energy, iron will in my career situations. Since I am a woman, the card may represent a father figure, which is true because it was my first impression of the man on the card. My fathers made me afraid of authority.

In the reversed position (card was upside down), indicates I need to be assertive, authoritative, and take leadership in solving the problem. In other situations, I may need to be less harsh. If in conflict, which I was at the university, I am justified in my beliefs, not to be blamed and will later achieve success. But I do long for better fairness and cooperation in higher education. Stressing over trying to survive a doctoral program didn't leave time nor energy to even think about love. Nor socializing. The author wrote that there is a possibility of the overthrowing tyrants and a new world order in this lifetime. My lifetime? And soon? That would be great!

Chapter 16: University: Triquetra Spread

I did a tarot card reading regarding delays in obtaining a practicum required for clinical training. When I read the tarot books' interpretation, the insight that was already coming to me, was validated. These cards were verifying what I was already seeing or intuiting that I had a question about but wasn't sure of.

Soon afterwards, I requested a private mediumship consultation at the Church of the Spirit with Dr. Ken James. An awesome reading so accurate and filled with connection energy that I forgot to record it. Although he didn't know my question or even that I was studying to be a psychologist, the messages that he brought through from spirit described my challenges at the university.

Later, I excitedly told Dr. Ken James that in the Holistic Tarot book, I discovered a section on using the Triquetra spread, that is used when previous tarot card consultations indicate ongoing problems. It helps give guidance on what inner growth, changes and divine interventions are needed to improve the situation. Simply, doing the Triquetra reading also has a spiritual component of being a prayer that energetically opens the way internally and externally. The interpretation of the cards I previously pulled with my eyes closed from the tarot card deck was similar to his mediumship message for me.

Signifier Card: Queen of Swords. Note: I chose the Queen of Swords as my signifier card because in a situation at the university I needed to confront an African American teacher who seemed to make it harder for African American students. He had a history of not making clear his expectations for written assignments for all the students in the courses he taught. Perhaps he had been there too long and didn't realize he had simplified his instructions too much. Plus, as he was the teacher who interviewed me and denied my admission to the doctoral program twenty years ago, when I was up walking but a little wobbly.

This was a required diversity class that showed us mostly videos about slavery, portrayal of "negros" in the old movies, and a few videos about the other three "people of color" groups in the United States — the Native Americans, Asian Americans, and Latino Americans. Each student had to make a list of all the stereotypes we had about each of these "minority" groups. Except that we were not allowed to list stereotypes we had about white people! Yet, African American students had to list stereotypes about other African Americans.

Card 1 Hangman XII Self-Sacrifice. Card 1 is the traits to focus on first and master the qualities. Advice: Need to yield to the greater good. You are tasked with the grave responsibility of sacrificing yourself for others. The mob has hung you because they do not approve of your beliefs or what you have done. But you are right, so you must trust yourself. You have wisdom, enlightenment, divine knowledge with what is good. Your different perspective offends the masses and so they prosecute you. But you do not need their approval. Hang in there. Also you have gained spiritual growth and innate prophesizing ability. You must forgive those who have condemned you. Must make a sacrifice for the greater good of the world.

Card 2 The Emperor: IV Authority. Card 2 is the traits you can master with the support of others and must ask for help with. Advice: You must wield great authority. Be commanding. Be demanding. Be a leader. Strong leadership skills are crucial to resolving your problems.

Card 3: The High Priestess II Intuition. Card 3 points out an important trait but is the most elusive to you. Therefore you must devote extra willpower to it. Advice: You have very good intuition. Use it. In making decisions involving the issue, go with the gut instinct. Represents spirituality, psychic energy and intuition, keeper of science, wisdom and knowledge. You must activate your intuition to retrieve this powerful unconscious knowledge, memory, and ability to encode, store and retrieve your experiences. Keep sensitive information secret for now and do not tell others yet. But be prepared to advance if needed at any moment, and appear calm and serene. An accomplished woman who strives to excel in a male-dominated institution. Using the command of personal femininity over yang or male dominant setting.

Chapter 17: University: Personal Reflections on the Meaning

I'd been living the depressed mood of the Nine of Swords since the fall semester. I've since read that the Queen of Swords is able to bear her sorrows, a lot of sorrows, and courageously speaks up, so I now know this was a good choice for the signifier card. Although I've pulled the Nine of Swords twice previously and I knew that it says it's not my fault, I would still question myself. Automatic ruminating, which I had not done before, especially at night caused insomnia. Questioned myself, asking if I did the right thing or said the right things. The teacher demanded honesty yet took issue with my honest sharing and advocating in my written assignments in the diversity class. How could I have written my papers differently? Why did I stay in the program anyway and be the victim? I lost my appetite. Some days I didn't feel like doing anything. Like how much more could I endure?

Interestingly, I pulled these cards for the Triquetra spread a few days before I was to meet with the two co-teachers for the diversity class. The tarot reading helped me to cope and know what to do with the meeting. I did end up having to take a leadership role in order to keep the meeting focused on specific goals, such as asking them to give me feedback and guidelines for revising my paper in writing (The Emperor). They wanted me to share more of my personal history which I had refrained from doing in the diversity training class with my peers during group because there are some students who gossip. I would have shared some more with the teachers at the meeting, except they kept insisting on their own assumptions and I saw they would not have understood. Under pressure, I started to get whiny and then remembered the High Priestess card advice not to share my secrets, to stay calm/serene, to take the lead and be demanding.

A couple of weeks later, I received notice that I was to have remediation. I had remediation before that held me back a year from my therapy practicum. Instead I was assigned to do clinical training in the university counseling center. I did well there, enjoyed having clients and supportive classmates and teachers, learning how to administer the MMPI, PIA, and other brief diagnostic questionnaires. My written reports were fine, versus the original teacher who sent me to remediation grading of a previous report that had so many red ink marks that you could barely see what I typed! I quietly put it in my file drawer at home and didn't ever look at it again. What good was all those red marks without explanations of how to make corrections?

Now I am sentenced me to eight sessions of biweekly remediation. That was my punishment (Hangman card). The dreaded remediation that was every diversity student's worst fear. We trembled through each class carefully choosing each word — oral and written. Since the multicultural diversity class was psychological torture for all the students we could not imagine what remediation would be like, nor having to repeat the class!

I appealed to the two deans and was still sentenced to remediation. They assigned me to one-on-one sessions with a South Asian diversity teacher. He was nice enough, mostly giving me reflective questions to answer about my experience in the diversity class as well as, a Black older woman who used a wheelchair, while he waited for the African American teacher to tell him the reason and goals for the remediation. Halfway through we didn't know. He stalled on asking the initial teachers because he, like the other teachers, did not agree but were afraid to confront his colleagues (hence as Dr. James' spirit message in April predicted, there would be a split).

The way the diversity class was structured and with the threat of having to repeat the class or remediation was an unjust practice that I spoke up against. Students before me should have never gone through and that no other students after me should never go through this (Hangman card). What was tricky was, I mostly just knew it was wrong, because of what one of the teacher's underlying attitude was, but could not explain it easily in words (hence the tarot advice to trust my intuition anyway).

Answering the assigned questions was cathartic allowing me to get my anger out on paper. He also asked for suggestions for improvements, which he later told me was implemented into the curriculum.

Another wonderful side of this, is that although I had to go through this emotional pain, Spirit provided guidance and support along the way, both from other people and with scholarly journal articles, books, and videos to share with the teachers to support my points (Card 2). The hardest was learning how to ask for help. From childhood, I'd became over independent (Queen of Swords). Now all of my childhood defense mechanisms, that were no longer needed, were being challenged for me to heal and let go. My core feelings of abandonment and isolation now made me desperate to be heard and acknowledged. I was not allowed to be angry and resentful as a child, or as a woman, so initially I turned the anger and fear inward onto myself as depression. Having to feel the anger and resentment now, as the 9 of Swords advised was painful, and made it difficult to forgive the teachers (Hangman card).

Much of what the two teachers did was from ignorance, not knowing what to do with a student who used a wheelchair, who was also older with rich life experiences, honest, and was culturally aware. Intellectually, I could rationalize their behavior but emotionally it was hard. In previous years at the predominantly white university, I fought silently with much inner conflict trying to hold onto who I was inside. Culturally, spiritually, and as a woman I valued relationships, emotions, interdependence, and intuition. The too many left-brain competitive activities of graduate school often had me feel cut off from myself and the world. So eventually, I reached a bursting point where I had to speak up and share of my culture when appropriate. Gratefully that semester, my other teachers were very supportive and encouraged me to share. So I regained my confidence over the long process. But over proving and defending myself had become a habit that, yes it was time to let go of, and ask or demand that others take up their responsibilities in changing the educational environment.

Personally I think it was the university's strategy to protect the university from losing accreditation because they weren't supposed to be enrolling more students than there were available clinical training sites. Black and older students were less likely to get matched to a clinic. In addition, the state's lack of adequate funding closed down many of the mental health clinics and agencies in the inner cities.

When I finally got a therapy practicum in a far away suburb, there were potential clients that were allowed to refuse to have a Black therapist. Unfair because Black patients don't have the luxury of being able to choose the skin complexion color of their medical doctors, nurses or therapists since colleges make sure they don't enroll, maintain, or graduate enough Black professionals. We are not dumb. We excel in most of what we do.

***

A friend called me and said "I just pulled the Seven of Swords from the African American tarot cards deck. I'm confused. When I look at the card, I see a man throwing the swords. The African-American card interpretation is about deception."

I read the interpretation from the [Holistic Tarot book](). What caught my attention was when the Nine of Swords card is reversed which I hope is happening for me now, then I would be in the healing stage as the emotional pain from a sense of loss is decreasing. I was beginning to see the overall situation. In time, I would be starting to hope that the worst is almost over.

"Wait a minute. I thought you said Seven of Swords."

"No, I meant the Nine of Swords. The African American tarot deck shows a man with a sword on both sides and on his back as he's pulling a sword out. But I don't understand these little pictures of African Americans at all. This one shows a man chasing someone out of his store who may have stolen something."

I said, "I thought that little picture is in the left corner of the cards was to represent famous Black people."

She said, "I don't know. It may be a famous person. I don't get it."

I said, "I do. I've been living the Nine of Swords. Yesterday I was crying and depressed same as I have been for two months."

She said, "You have?"

"Yes, I have been, although I know that it says it's not my fault. I still go there and feel guilty. Last week, my therapist reminded me of that, even though I didn't say I was blaming myself. She knew. I just automatically go to question myself whether I did the right thing or said the right thing. I like the African American cards better. They fight back. Not just sit on the bed in the dark, depressed, with the window blinds closed. Even the man chasing after the other person is fighting back! Thank you very much for sharing that. You made my day!"

She said, "I did?"

I said, "Yes, you did. I don't know how the card applies to your life, but it certainly has been my life for most of 2015. Similar to with my I Ching and solstice readings. I rarely know how the readings will play out. I don't know what they mean until later."

The next day I called my sister on my cell phone, while I was in the paratransit van on my way to the university. I said, "Remember I got the Queen of Swords last year at the beginning of 2015. I didn't know what it meant at the time. Now after rereading it this week I get it. She's a bad ass queen. She is able to bear her sorrows."

She said "What?"

I said, "All in all I feel better this morning. I have more energy. But the worry and instant replay of scratched records had crept in from time to time. After I hung up the phone, I felt a tap on my shoulder. The young man's tap, sitting in the seat behind me in the van, broke through my thoughts.

"You'll be all right."

I wholeheartedly told him, "Thank you. That means a lot to me."

He could feel my worry. He understood.

Chapter 18: University: The Squeaky Wheel

Later in the day when I met with the assistant clinical training director, I found myself getting agitated. I had told myself I would be calm as I gently told him, "People are all just trying to stay afloat. Some practicum supervisors are worried that they won't be able to give me enough hours. They suggested that renewing my CRC or other counseling license may help."

He said, "So they can bill insurances."

I nodded as I continued, "My classmates have therapy practicums in the northern or far west suburbs because they have cars. I don't have transportation. I have to look at reality for what it is. I started asking for help last year and I'm asking again now, because we need to come up with strategies on how to do this. I can't do this by myself, although I'm sure tried. You saw me on Tuesday and commented on how bundled up I was. and asked me about the big bag of salt I was carrying for melting the ice. Now I have to carry a shovel and an ice pick with me. No one has shoveled out the bus stops. I talked to the security guards here at the entrance to the building leasing our university. One of the security guards told me, "It's the city's job to shovel the outer sidewalks."

Perhaps they are protesting because the mayor raised the property taxes. In all the years that I've been coming here, they've shoveled the sidewalks. To get on the bus to get here, I had to make a way through the hardened snow. This is my reality, as is with other people who have disabilities. I have friends neglected in nursing homes because the governor is holding back the budget and hasn't paid Medicaid bills in almost two years. The governor before him delayed payments six months out. Since 2008, with the Great Recession people lost their jobs and/or health insurance coverage. Therefore, a lot of local community mental health centers and hospitals were forced to close. So where am I to get my clinical training?"

The assistant clinical director of training's face was without smiles this whole time that I'm talking. None of his usual jokes or inserting music album lyrics and release dates. This made me angry because I felt he was still trying to push me to do more to get a practicum, as if I wasn't doing enough. I surprised myself and said while raising my voice a little, "I've been here too long. I'm starting to feel like a child gone wild and crazy."

I meant to say, "I feel like a neglected child that is left to run wild."

What I didn't know, as he walked me across the hall to fill out some forms, is that the new administrative assistant hadn't sent notices to my personal emails with updates to keep me informed of the practicum process due dates and forms. This was January, one important form was due back in October. She might have sent it to my campus email, but I was probably buried too deep in class assignments, and partially immobilized with depression and emotional pain from the diversity class and having to do an unfair remediation.

The next week it snowed again. From home, I called the management company office requesting that they shovel. The person who answered the phone said, "Another person in another department handles that. And he doesn't get in until 8:30 AM."

I gave her my name, phone number and emphasized that I use a wheelchair. A few minutes later, on the website I saw the contact emails for the property manager, so I wrote him the following:

"Will you see that the sidewalks are shoveled all the way out to the curb? For those of us that use wheelchairs, walkers, canes, etc. we need to be able to get out from vehicles onto the sidewalks. And the buses and special paratransit vans need to be able to let down the ramp flat onto the sidewalk. The area around the bus shelter needs to have a clear wide path."

As an afterthought, I ccd the assistant clinical training director, who responded immediately. He forwarded the email to the student services department. When I arrived to school at 10:30 AM every inch of the sidewalk was cleared along with the entire plaza area, which at 12 degrees air temperature no one would be sitting outside anyway. However hundreds of people cross the plaza to get to the main entrance of the building because the Metra Millennium train station is located in the lower levels. To say I was immensely impressed is an understatement.

CHAPTER 18: UNIVERSITY: THE SQUEAKY WHEEL

Unfortunately, the path to getting me an internship was not cleared as fast. In fact, even with some faculty teachers trying to help from behind the scenes, others added more storms and obstacles. I was on my own, as most staff gave up trying because the few usual avenues they attempted went nowhere. The problem is that often you don't find out that your request didn't go anywhere until weeks later! Welcome to what the world is like for people with disabilities.

An abrupt realization came to me, I would have to constantly tell everyone what using a wheelchair and otherwise having a disability is like. As other people with disabilities will testify, we explain but people conveniently forget. Every moment would have to be a "teachable moment." My therapist introduced me to the terms "teachable moments" and "picking one's battles." However, all the burden becomes on me to decide when it is a teachable moment, and when it is a battle worth fighting at that particular moment. All the consequences are also all on me for whatever of these decisions I make. Doesn't the power differential matter with me being the student, and them being the teachers who decide my grades and my fate based on how much I cooperate and don't make waves?

Therefore, should I have been the "squeaky wheel" sooner as my academic advisor told me.

He told me to, "You have to bug the training department every two weeks because it's the squeaky wheel that gets results."

What was I to do when they had me bogged down with irrelevant stupid aggravations that took up most of my time? When the training department staff changed almost every year? Yet, the deans were the same. And they always ask, "How may I help you?" Really?

I did go to them again and again, but as with customer service phone calls, their replies and recommendations are prepared scripts that they tell to everyone. Or put you on hold, sometimes indefinitely, so after a while you just hang up. Somehow, even in person they see, but don't see that I am in front of them in a wheelchair. Especially when upon arrival, they tell me, "Have a seat, I'll be with you in a minute."

Thus, if I didn't squeak enough it was my fault? I understand the concrete barriers such as stairs and walls, but I don't know if I'll ever understand the human attitudinal barriers. After a while, I couldn't care about graduate school anymore. Certainly not to put all my energies into it. In order to survive, I began to develop my interests and sense of belonging elsewhere. I submerged myself into Black community activities, developed my spiritual abilities, and designed knitted winter accessories.

The knitting served two purposes for me: one) a sense of accomplishment in doing something right, contrary to the University making me feel "all wrong" with their unpredictable expectations, and two) by making complicated knitting patterns my mind was occupied in a positive way instead of being obsessed twenty-four seven with the constant replays of what the teachers said, or what I could've said, or what I did say and then regretted.

Did I even want to be a psychologist when my teachers treated students and each other in such uncaring ways? After all, aren't psychologists supposed to study and understand human behavior so as to empathetically help others? Would I be pressured just to graduate or have a job in this profession to behave the same way? Do we ignore the realities of everyday life and pretend we are safe as long as we are high up inside the ivory tower of academia? I refuse to numb myself and go back to being a zombie, alive but a walking dead inside. Almost 30 years ago when my abusive husband took almost everything away from me: my family, friends, job, home and then when my cupboards and bank account were bare he moved on. On the verge of losing my soul too, I vowed then not to let anyone try to steal my soul. The shock of this memory and its similarity to the abusive situation at the university woke me up to my aliveness. Being alive meant being awakened to the painful truth of what was happening around me and to me.

Chapter 19: What if There is a Fire?

We were in a staffing meeting, on the fourth floor, when the alarms sounded. I listened for the number of bells to try to determine what type of danger or drill. Our supervisor was leading the staff meeting and asked us which alarm it was. He said, "Fire alarm. Do you know what to do?"

He then directed us to evacuate. I stopped my wheelchair at the entrance to the main stairs, watching everyone go down the stairs except the supervisor and me.

"Where is the fire marshal?" I asked.

"Do you know what to do?"

I started to say, 'In all the drills I've been in I was told to wait in my wheelchair at the top of the stairs.'

Previously, in preparation for a possible fire in my apartment building, I called 311 and asked what to do. They didn't know, instead recommended I call my local fire department. For a month, I searched for their number that used to always be in the front of the large white and yellow phone books, now not even online. Finally I asked some firemen at the Access Chicago Disability Expo at Navy Pier and they gave me a card with a fire department number on it. I called and she told me, "The firemen know where your apartment is, just stay there and they will come and get you."

I asked, "What if I'm visiting in another apartment, or in another area of the building?"

She repeated, "The fireman will know what to do."

While I was thinking about an answer for my supervisor, two male staff members appeared beside me. They were both tall and well-built. One older and stocky, the other young. The young one said he was an EMT. I asked him, "Then you know how to do the fireman's carry?"

He said, "Yes."

"With two people? It's easier with two people."

He told the older man to reach under me with first one arm and then the other, he did the same as they lifted me from my wheelchair. They slowly carried me down the stairs. There was heavy smoke on the second floor. We continued down the stairs with my knees up and gaped open, my back leaning backwards. I didn't feel like the men would drop me, it was just uncomfortable. Another man came and supported my back. When we got to the lobby they asked for a chair and sat me down on it. When the fireman came down to give the "all clear," one of the staff told me someone would bring my wheelchair down. From the lobby I saw the elevator door open and someone was calling my name, almost cussing as he struggled to steer the wheelchair to turn it in the direction he wanted, to get it out of the elevator doorway. I yelled, "Use two fingers. Just two fingers! Use a gentle touch!"

I was glad it was my old wheelchair. The older man didn't say anything much throughout our ordeal. I wondered if he thought I was being ungrateful and rude when I had asked earlier where the floor marshal was. And later commented that we took too long to get out of the building. We would have gotten burned up if it was a real fire. The EMT then said if it had been a real fire, he would have just slung me over his shoulder. I walked sideways from the chair to my power wheelchair with them holding me under my arms on both sides.

Later, the administrative assistant told me she called and looked for men to come and get me down the stairs. I expressed my gratitude. Other staff during the following week approached me and told me they were glad someone brought me downstairs, and others said they would have carried me down themselves. I felt loved and cared for by these responses.

It was an unsettling feeling to have almost everyone leave me on the fourth floor. I know it was a minor fire. But still! So much for the previous instructions I received in the Michigan Plaza building fire drill, where I had to wait at the top of the stairs for what was described to me, would be a soon to come, young, handsome, muscular firefighter. It was just in our imaginations. The drill was over soon, and no one had to carry me down thirteen flights of stairs of a downtown high-rise building. It's difficult emotionally to get past memories of September 11, 2001 and stories of people in wheelchairs left behind or a few heroically carried down.

When I arrived home that evening, I checked YouTube videos and saw that the "fireman's carry" is when the victim is slung over a fireman's shoulder. Years ago, one of my friends invited me to her house for Thanksgiving. She and a woman neighbor carried me very smoothly up and down her front stairs. The carry technique that they used is the "two person lift." According to the video, even a victim that's lying on the floor can be assisted into a standing position, to then sit on the two rescuers' linked arms. This would have given me a more secure ride.

Asking my apartment building manager and a security guard about their procedure for a fire wasn't much better. They laughed and said, "There are sprinklers in each apartment. If there were a fire, then there would be water flooding everywhere. You don't have to worry."

Well, I could take some consolation that maybe I wouldn't get burned up in the fire, but the water from the sprinklers would short out the electrical circuits on my wheelchair.

Chapter 20: Elevators Out

It happened. Time to go home and the elevators that were working two hours earlier, decided to stop working again. One was stuck in the basement and the other on the third floor. Emily did all the usual tricks to try to get the elevators to move. She went down to the third floor and pushed and pulled on the elevator door to get the door to close. It wouldn't budge.

My phone rang, "Ms Mateen, your ride is outside. They will only wait five minutes."

"Give me time to get downstairs. I'm on the fifth floor."

"We can only give you five minutes."

"They are 35 minutes late, and they can't wait five minutes for me! I've waited three hours or more for them on other days."

"Tell them to wait for you! Tell them we've got to have time to get down the stairs. We will need more than five minutes."

Emily led the way to the stairwell.

"We need to do the firemen carry. Two people can do it."

"I can't do all that. We'll help you. Josh you get in the front of her. I'll get in back of you on the side. Dr. Mateen, you hold onto the railing here. Come on we'll help you."

As I stood there, in my mind I'm starting to panic. What if this was a fire? Here we go again. People assume that since I can walk some that I can go up and down stairs. Even when I explain to my family and friends they still don't understand. This is why previously I've hid that I could stand up and walk. Even at the expense of my own self-humiliation as I allowed people to do for me what I could do for myself. Obviously, I've made a mistake that could one day cost my life, just so that I could be myself, my authentic self. People could respect me for being me, not a wheelchair.

A therapist coworker used a walker for walking long distances. However at the clinic she would go without her walker to get her clients from the waiting room. From then on, I did the same. I sat in a regular chair after parking my wheelchair in a corner of the large office room. I got better respect from other coworkers and clients. Although I would suffer after walking too much during the day, with awful pain in my back, and from my knees down to my toes at night, I was determined to graduate. But this is so wrong! Plenty people can't get up and walk, and like me they can do plenty more, and are very intelligent.

***

Memories of when I allowed well-meaning family members to convince me to go up and downstairs anyway. They were harder to get it in their heads that I couldn't do stairs because family are the ones who have seen me walk the most in houses where floors are flat and smooth. They too have told me, "You can do it. We'll help you get up the stairs."

And they did. However, my rotator cuff in my left shoulder was severely injured although two people were lifting and moving my legs up the stairs, because I was literally pulling myself along the side railings. People don't know that the same problem with the muscles in my legs being partially paralyzed, also happened to my upper arms. That was in an emergency situation, so I did it. Another time I didn't want to get embarrassed, or embarrass my sister and brother, or delay the small crowd of people waiting, and thought I was stronger, so I allowed my brother to intimidate me into climbing the stairs. I get severe back pain each time I try, going downstairs too, that lasts for days afterwards. Later my brother told me, with his head down and a sad look in his eyes that he had to struggle to hold my back up from behind. It was then that

I understood while I could move my legs better, I lacked core upper body strength control to hold myself upright.

"Let's go, Dr. Mateen. They are going to leave you."

I took one shaky step down. This was another emergency situation. Whatever has needed to be done I've done it. Pushed myself to just do it in the moment. Looking down the steep stairs to the landing, I remember thinking many times in the past that in an emergency my legs would just automatically work. I've been practicing walking longer and longer at the office and walking heel-to-toe forward instead of sideways. At home doing my Qigong exercises, which to my surprise was strengthening my core, so that for example I have been able to stand longer at my kitchen sink washing and rinsing dishes with less sharp pains in my upper back. I still had to pace myself because having my hands in moderately warm water would make all of my muscles weak. Same if the room was too hot or too cold. Here we were standing at the top of the stairs in a cold hallway on the fifth floor. It was much shorter flights of stairs that I tried to navigate years ago. How could I do five or more flights of stairs going down?

I got my answer for sure, as I decided not to do it, I turned and struggled to lift my leg up the one step. We walked the short hallway back into the office.

A coworker looking out the window said, "The van pulled off already."

The rest of my coworkers gathered around me in the large office waiting room. Everyone talking all at once, in a dazed atmosphere of confusion. We put our heads together to come up with solutions.

I felt helpless. None of the solutions seem to make sense. They've waited with me before, as Pace paratransit would almost strand me if I hadn't been able to keep calling Pace on my cell phone. Learned the hard way that if I didn't schedule my ride home before 3:00 PM, the drivers could be three or more hours late to get me from the office, not to mention the other two hours ride to my home as they picked up and dropped off and picked up and dropped off other passengers along the way. Drivers have "no showed me" gone off leaving me, without giving me the courtesy call to let me know they were there and give me time to come down from the fifth floor. Dispatch would then say they didn't have any rides available for several hours.

If someone else gave me a ride home, I would have to leave my wheelchair at the office. Up until now, I haven't had to do that. I've been practicing my walking just in case, thinking maybe it would be okay if I had to. But why did it have to happen on Wednesday? The office was closed on Thursdays. On a hybrid schedule, I wasn't due back to work until Monday. How would I get to the grocery store or other places outside to take care of business? Even if I ordered groceries, ever since the COVID pandemic whoever delivers food leaves the bags downstairs in the lobby. They are doing construction on the first floor of my building. Management staff is rarely in the office.

But I still had to get downstairs to go home. Calling the fire department was a suggestion. But what if the firemen came right away, since the firehouse was only a few blocks away? Still didn't know how long I would have to wait for a ride home. Would the firemen carry my over 300 pound wheelchair down five flights of stairs? If not, was the new sidewalk to my building flat enough so I could walk across, to the elevators, and to my apartment when I got there?

So many questions and possibilities. Instead of continuing to guess, I decided to call and find out what our options were with the fire department.

I called 311 because this was a non-emergency call. No one answered. It was 4:30 in the afternoon the staff probably went home. So I called

CHAPTER 20: ELEVATORS OUT

911 immediately saying, "This is a non-emergency call. The elevators are not working. I need help getting downstairs."

"To where?"

Puzzled, I said, "Downstairs to the first floor."

"We only take people downstairs to go to medical appointments."

This I didn't understand. Many of my friends who use wheelchairs have fallen in their homes, and often called the fire department to help them get off the floor and positioned back into their wheelchair or bed. I've never had to call the fire department for help before. So I didn't know their procedures.

A coworker grabbed my phone and said loudly, "She uses a wheelchair. The elevators are not working. She needs to get down to the first floor. The first floor!"

The call-taker transferred the call. A deep husky voice said, "Have the door open for us."

Neither one of them allowed me to explain or get more information from them. So much for that idea. Within ten minutes, my phone rang, "We're downstairs. The doors are locked, how do we get in?

Two firemen arrived with their special seat. It reminded me of the ultrathin transport aisle chairs used on airplanes. I'm thin, but I can't imagine how anyone bigger than I am, fits on the seat and be comfortable. The firemen looked at me, and looked at my motorized wheelchair, scratched their heads and then said, "No, we can't carry that down."

One fireman came by me, asking me my name and birthdate. If my coworkers didn't know my age, now they do. "How do you spell it" as he tried to write it on his blue exam gloves. I said, "Here give me the pen. It will be easier for me to just write it."

Unknown to me, outside in the hallway were several other firemen trying to fix the elevator. We heard a loud, "Hurray." It would be great if they have the elevators fixed and this saga over with. But then disappointment as the elevator still didn't move.

To my relief, four fireman helped carry me down the stairs. Two firemen in front holding handles on each side and two firemen in the back holding handles on each side of the special seat. As I waited while they position themselves, I told myself not to think about the times that I've almost been dropped. Trusting that it will be fine since there were now four men carrying me instead of one or two. They only rested very briefly when setting the chair down on each landing to make the turn to go down the next flight of stairs. They didn't moan and groan. We were downstairs quickly.

The same fireman stayed by my side the whole time. This was comforting. In the building entrance lobby downstairs, near tears I told him, "I'm remembering all the times I didn't have the patience to wait for in line for slow crowded elevators. I would simply run up the stairs two steps at a time as if it was no thing!"

I didn't realize how shook up I was until I tried to do simple things while sitting downstairs waiting for a ride home. Like recalling people's names and forgetting I already had other information in my phone but asking others. It was difficult for me to concentrate. Grateful that my boss sat next to me, and other coworkers stayed past their usual work hours. It would be days later, after the shock gradually were off, that I realize how traumatic, re-traumatizing the whole event was. How terrifying having to totally depend on others, was triggering for me. I still didn't know how to fully trust and accept help.

Hadn't even remembered that I hadn't taken my muscle spasm medicine baclofen since very early in the morning. I thought my legs were stiff as I walked on the sidewalk to the car because I had been sitting for an hour waiting in the cold hallway lobby.

And of course, during the night my mind kept going over what happened. Maybe all of this happened because a couple years ago I prayed for complete healing. Heaven graciously conspired to gradually have me without my wheelchairs. My current power chair needs new batteries, and the armrest is dangling when it should be giving my left arm and shoulder support thus reducing shoulder pain. Actually it's time for a whole new wheelchair but may be too expensive for me to afford. Do I even want a $30,000 wheelchair if I'm being shown that I may not need it anymore?

My portable fold-up, fit in the trunk of a car travel electric wheelchair got broken during the move while my apartment was been remodeled. Now I don't have a backup wheelchair. The movers left boxes stacked everywhere so I couldn't use a wheelchair in my apartment anyway. Therefore I had to do more walking.

Plus, recently I've had nightmares of unconsciously walking away from my wheelchair at large conference events, and then having to walk to find where I left it hours later when it was time for me to go home. Other nightmares of being on public city buses and being distracted while talking to someone else. Jumping off the bus at an unknown bus stop, only realizing later after the bus pulled off that I left my wheelchair with my jacket, purse, everything. Dream interpretation books indicate wallets and purses symbolize personal identity.

Since the COVID pandemic, we've all had ongoing multiple crises which kind of force us to let go of our old identities, and ways of thinking and doing. I've certainly changed a lot so I was hoping that leaving behind my wheelchair was just symbolic. Just in case this becomes real, I started strapping my heavy fanny pack to my waist.

Here in the daytime, I actually walked away from my wheelchair. It was no longer a just a dream. Left it at the office. Calmly not thinking about how people have broken my wheelchairs in the past. I had to fully trust that all would be well. Because yes my wheelchair has become an almost invisible extension of myself. Very much a part of my identity after twenty years.

PART THREE: HEALING

Chapter 21: Other Aspects of Auset

During the Ausar Auset Society Church's meditations to achieve a goal, including spiritual growth goals during the solstices, we were instructed to start with Auset at the bottom of the Tree of Life and go up, one-by-one for each deity to Ausar near the top. Doing the Auset meditations, with seeing ourselves being held and breastfed by Mother, was intended to take us back to memories that our habits and childhood conditioning originated from. Allowing the memories to surface, along with the feelings to help us release and heal the past, so we could move forward in our lives.

Until reviewing my life now, as I write this second book, it hadn't occurred to me that my multiple years of receiving counseling and psychotherapy was probably a continuation of the Auset healing that began in Zimbabwe. There they nurtured and cared for me similar to how families determine every need and give instructions to a young child. In a foreign country, not knowing the language nor culture, what else could I do? Heaven knew that otherwise I would have resisted this care, and I did resist when I returned to the United States and became ill and unemployed.

Special Prayers and Miracles from Great Mother Auset Yemeja Azna

I learned of the power of Great Mother Azna in 2004, when I was reading Silvia Browne's books about being a psychic medium, interpreting dreams, where she vaguely mentioned choosing from a list of archetype type categories that she titles "life themes" that we each agreed to before we are born. I wanted to know more about the life themes and came upon her book, <u>Mother God: The Feminine Principle to Our Creator.</u>

Although I knew about the mother deity personas of Auset and Yemeja since 1991, and did rituals with Auset's mantras and meditations, somehow I had not thought to pray to Her directly. When you think about it, unless you had an abusive mother, more often you went to your mother when you wanted something or when you were in trouble. Your father was more likely to say, "No." Or be too busy. There are many stories about people when they were about to die called out to their mothers first and then to God. So why not me?

I followed the instructions in the book, <u>Mother God</u>, for petitioning Great Mother Azna to say aloud specifically what I wanted, including a timeframe of when, then ask for a sign. Answers can be subtle and come from different sources such as new ideas and opportunities. Great Mother Azna tends to send flowers to acknowledge that She heard your prayers. The flowers She sent me were red geraniums, and a small houseplant of tiny red roses. Usually soon afterwards your wish is granted. In brief relaxation meditations, She shows me a garden of red roses in bright, vivid colors, while giving me a warm feeling of peace and love. Later that day I receive an answer to my prayers. But sometimes it takes much longer. Long enough for me to have forgotten my request and when I made it.

I reserve special tough requests for Great Mother. Simply my choice, She fixes small problems too, but since She is known for granting miracles, miracles is what I ask for. I talk to Her aloud. I prayed a lot to Great Mother while trying to survive the Supportive Living situation. Eventually, of course, I got brave enough to want full healing.

When I got tired of having to wear three different incontinence products

— a diaper, pull-up, and thick pad all together, and these still weren't enough to hold my urine — I cried out to Great Mother for help. I had to change them at least six times a day when I was away from home. Incontinence supply companies shipped a month's worth of supplies in large boxes that filled my closet, lower bookshelves, nightstand, behind and underneath my bed. Space where I could have put my clothes and craft items. I had no bladder control, especially when I was too cold or too hot. Could not drink carbonated sodas or coffee without the floodgates opening, peeing nonstop. Honestly, I don't know how other people get away with drinking that stuff all day. The physical therapist had me doing Kegel exercises, which she applauded since I did them well, yet became disappointed because when

I was trying to get up from the physical therapy mat, out came my urine. The problem was during changing positions from lying or sitting to standing is my brain couldn't tell my legs what to do and my bladder perineum muscles how to tightly close, and do both at the same time. Medically I shouldn't have been able to move my legs at all to transfer to the wheelchair, or to walk. I had to mentally will my legs to move.

First, Great Mother made me allergic to the absorbent gel inside the pads causing me to break out in rashes and blisters. Then I stopped urinating as frequently at night, noticing my bed would be dry in the morning. With time, I was making it to the toilet on time without even a dribble. The only time I had accidents was when

I was like a kid that doesn't want to stop whatever I was doing.

The next miracle I asked of Great Mother was to not have to use a ventilator at night to breath. My neurologist diagnosed me with both central sleep apnea and obstructive sleep apnea. Central sleep apnea is when the brain forgets to tell the diaphragm breathing muscles to breathe. I was gasping for air whenever I started to nod off to sleep and through the night. So instead of a continuous positive air pressure (CPAP) machine for snoring, I had a variable positive air pressure (VPAP) machine that was set at a specified rate and rhythm to breath for me whenever I stopped breathing. During the Great Recession's early years many companies closed, including respiratory supply companies. In addition, some specialists at hospitals stopped taking patients who had Medicare insurance. My primary care doctor did what she could to get me supplies, however without respiratory therapists and pulmonologists who specialized in neuromuscular diseases, there was no one to reset my VPAP machine as my condition changed. If I gained or lost weight the mask no longer fits, and neither did the rhythm match my breathing rate anymore. It was as if I was fighting against the machine plus the cold air hurting my nose and the back of my throat was incredibly painful. So gradually, I ditched using the VPAP machine. And I did alright without it.

It took years for me to get brave enough to ask Great Mother for my arms and legs to be healed. This would mean a huge change in lifestyle and thinking. All of my requests were answered gradually over time. When the airline broke the back of my wheelchair, severe back pain kept me from sitting in it for long periods, so I had to get up and move to relieve the pain. My apartment kitchen was too small to turn my wheelchair around in, so I had to stand and hold on to the kitchen counter. Initially I was tired and dizzy but gradually could stand longer and longer enough to prepare meals. Gradually my back and knees didn't hurt so much during the day from trying to walk, and took less revenge at night. I had less stomach troubles with constipation, as being upright allowed gravity and exercise to aid proper digestion. One day, I will return for another bone density test that will show my bones are healthier too.

Chapter 22: Be Careful What You Ask For

There is a saying, "be careful what you ask for because you just might get it!" Let me tell you the story of a friend who been praying and praying, including doing rituals to Osun to lose weight. Soon afterwards, her rent was raised. Police put a boot lock on the wheel of her car because of her daughter's old unpaid parking tickets. This meant she had to walk to the grocery store three blocks away and walk to the bus stops, instead of drive. Then her credit card accounts were closed, which stopped her from using her credit cards to eat out or order restaurant home deliveries. She was angry, feeling unfairly inconvenienced, and got mad at God because she believed that it must be evil things happening to her! Hey, her prayers were answered. Quick, fast and in a hurry. What more did she want?

We get comfortable in our routines, make resolutions to change but excuses and events get in the way, and/or we often don't know what is truly involved in order for our prayers to be answered. So our spirit guides force the issue by giving us real life experiences to teach us what we need to know in order to have what we want. Perhaps they get tired of us nagging them and say, "Here, here take it! Are you really sure that's what you want?"

Some of us don't know when we are receiving a gift or will try to give it back.

Ungrateful, we would rather return to old routines and continued crises.

Prayers are answered, but sometimes it may not seem like it because although the Bible says, "ask and you shall receive," people don't always listen and follow guidance given to them from spirit. Results may be delayed because a person is not using their gifts and talents the person was born with and are not on their own destiny path. Instead, they are trying to follow someone else's expectations. When you are on your own destiny path, life flows synchronistically with all the items and people available to help you.

Another important reason prayers may not seem to be answered, is when you are being prepared to be able to receive, or to carry out the duties of the role or job you were praying for. You want to get married or find the ideal companion. But do you even know what love, or a healthy relationship is? Most people don't know what love is, because we weren't taught in our families, schools, nor communities. Learning love is a process that occurs over a lifetime. Each encounter with another person or being, is an opportunity to accept and learn about love. Sometimes we have to experience what love is not, in order to desire and learn what real love is. The same with careers and personal talents.

We have choices, when we are at a crossroads. I like to call these situations "life detours" and use the analogy of being on a highway. With ongoing construction at different times of our lives, we are forced to or have the opportunity to take a different road. You may discover that this different side-road is even faster. You might find what you have been needing or wanting along the way. You meet people who may share stories, information and directions that provide answers or a different way of relating. Perhaps you will experience new beauty and fun.

Or you may come to a dead-end road and have to figure out how to turn around, and get back on your journey. Some people choose to stay on the highway with the construction or poor road conditions because either other options were not available, or they were determined to take risks, or they were half asleep and missed the warning signs. Sometimes they may end up stuck in a rut, but eventually get out. This may seem to take some extra frustrating time, but when you look back on your life years later, you'll see you were still traveling in the direction of your initial personal goals or destination. Each detour scenario gives you a different perspective on your life. Therefore acquiring more strength, knowledge, and self-esteem along with your new abilities to now understand and accept your prayers being answered.

Overtime I added to my aligning my hara line morning prayer ritual. After reading, <u>Mystical Traveler,</u> also by Silvia Browne, I say, 'I align my I Am' with divine rays and allow divine rays to flow through my rays. I also allow Great Mother's rays to flow through my rays." To this I later added, "I remember, love, respect, and honor you Great Mother. As above, so below, restoring balance to the world. Bringing back true love, peace, harmony, and unity. I'm open to assisting, and experiencing you Great Mother, the yin in all that is. Including experiencing the yin in those who have chosen male or yang energy bodies. Bringing back our acceptance of our emotions which is our connection to all that is as One. My heart is opened to being love, experiencing love, learning love, sharing as well as receiving true love. I ask that all that is — everywhere — has plenty of safe and healthy food, safe and healthy resources, and most importantly safe and healthy environments filled with divine true love, peace, harmony and unity within each of us and within all that is."

When I do this morning prayer, my whole day flows smoothly with love and caring, as other people also offer their presence or help.

Our emotions and intuition are the foundation of healthy relationships as we feel and know what our loved ones and others are feeling and thinking. There was a time, before colonization when it was not possible to lie to ourselves or to others. We were energetically connected to each other as One and telepathy was natural. Emotions give us the passionate energy to follow through on creative ideas, to fulfill our true potential individually and most importantly together as a universe. Father God has been hiding away from us for a long time, afraid of His emotions and true unconditional loving intimate relationships, He pushed Mother God and Her emotions away. Well, She now has the courage to step forth and make Her presence known. Restoring balance to the world.

Chapter 23: Mother Mary in Africa

What further had me fall completely in love with Great Mother was reading the book, <u>Our Lady of Kibeho: Mary Speaks to the World from the Heart of Africa.</u> Mother Mary, also known as the Virgin Mary, appeared as spirit apparitions that only a few Catholic school children could see. She was real to them. They would spontaneously go into trance with their eyes looking upwards and relay Mother Mary's messages. Most of the messages were given through songs that were about the need to repent, love and care for each other. Starting months apart, this happened first to one of the girls and then later another girl. The school, church, and other officials didn't believe them, and initially bullied and punished the girls. However, as word got out the children drew crowds of people who witnessed the holy visitations and experienced the overwhelming peace, joy, love and miracles as the public also received healing of their illnesses or injuries, and given whatever else they asked for. All Mother Mary required was that they pray with a rosary, and most importantly love each other, forgive themselves and their neighbors by not holding even a tiny bit of animosity in their hearts. Villagers fed and cared for those who made the pilgrimage from other cities and countries. The messages and miracles continued for several years during the 12 years before the genocide in Rwanda. The genocide happened because some people didn't heed Mother Mary's patient warnings and later very descriptive visions of pools of blood warnings of what could happen, if they did not purge their hearts of malice.

In her later book, <u>Left to Tell</u>, Immaculee Ilibagiza tells stories of surviving the actual genocide. It was her silent prayers to Mother Mary that saved her. The intense energy of love, along with her silent prayers confused the would-be killers, because they were expecting her to be afraid. It was as if she temporally became invisible to them. Thereafter, Mother Mary led Immaculee to places of safety, comforted her in the loss of her family, helped her form new relationships and careers.

One Sunday, as I meditated with Great Mother at the Church of the Spirit, beyond my half closed eyes I saw a large light blue glow in the middle of the front of the church. Later during the service, I noticed many women were wearing turquoise blue that day. I wondered if there were and are many other sightings of the Mother, and why She was reminding me of Her presence so often and strongly. What message is She needing to get through our thick heads?

In my brief exposure to Christianity as a child, in the Bible and multiple readings of the Quran although there is the story of the Virgin Mary giving birth to Jesus, afterwards the emphasis is only on his life, and his ability to perform miracles. His mother's ability to manifest miracles was omitted. He acquired some awesome genes and had a great role-model. People prayed to him and the Father, but I hadn't heard of people praying to the Virgin Mary. I knew Catholics had Saints and that there were many statues of the Virgin Mary, but I have not studied Catholicism.

Over the centuries, Mother Mary appeared to many children and people who did not know of her or had no religious exposure at all. She brings warnings and comfort. Unfortunately, leaders who wanted to keep "power," publicly accused the children of lying so that wars and other wrongdoing could continue. I believe Immaculee Ilibagiza's incredible stories are true because I witnessed Great Mother's miracles in my own life before I read her books. I'm very grateful for Great Mother healing me.

Chapter 24 Wisdom Gained

Having a disability taught me a lot. It helped me think outside of the box because I had to compensate and solve problems and tasks in a completely different way than I had learned coming up, from most people I knew. If I don't try new ways now, I would be like many of my friends with disabilities stuck in their homes. And I was determined not to go into a nursing home.

The reason I can walk at all is because I walk sideways, like a crab. I moved my legs forward stiffly from my hips, since I have difficulty lifting my knees to pull up the rest of my lower legs. Proximal weakness, meaning the quadriceps muscles in my thighs struggled do their job. For me, trying to walk forward had me tripping over my own feet, almost falling. I catch myself by jerking upright hurting my back. Walking devices — such as canes and walkers — are made for people to walk forward like everybody else. Well, me being different shouldn't be a surprise. What's beautiful is that I did teach myself to walk. Although sideways, it's walking! I can get across a room quickly, so quickly that people don't notice that I'm walking sideways. Walking backwards is also easier, except I can't see where I'm going. If my head could turn 360 degrees, then I'd be alright!

In the rest of my life I've also learned to compensate, adapt, and be okay with doing things very different than other people. What does it matter how a task is done as long as the goal is accomplished?

You May be Wondering . . .

What do I believe in? Over my lifetime, I've noticed it doesn't matter what belief or religion I've explored, the universe still provides for me guidance and abundance. Has shown me miracles in the midst of crises, therefore ever increasing my faith. Faith may be the key to healing — faith that life can be better. Of course I've also done my part to improve and maintain my health. It makes better sense to be aware of your body, mind and spirit as well as the effect of the environment. What does your body need in order to be in balanced harmony? What has illnesses and crises taught you, that has given you a better quality of life with increasing inner satisfaction?

Much of what we learn in life is from experience. In regards to religions, holy books, and rules, I'm gaining a deeper understanding of their initial intent and meaning. The natural innocence of young children, indigenous and gnostic beliefs before the major religions forced dominance over truth and peace. Personally, I prefer to say, Great Mystery, Great Spirit, Pure Love, and or maybe Infinite Intelligence within all instead of "God" because no one knows for sure how the universe functions. So why argue? We could all do our part as humans co-creators to have healthy and safe environments for all.

Books and Articles

I purposely did not write this book in a scholarly way, with huge academic words, book quotes and citations. This is because we all have this knowledge and information within us. Books are just one way to share and communicate with each other. I believe there really is no such thing as an expert, it is simply one person sharing their opinion and experiences. The so-called expert may have done the research and statistics to find how many other people might agree. And they had the money and the time to get published. But life is always changing. Meaning what was true two weeks ago, may not be true today. And the authors may live in a completely different situation than yours, and therefore the advice may make no sense for your current life situation. Books are a way to have a long-distance conversation. Often with a stranger. But there is enough commonalities so that we don't feel alone. Here is a list of books whose authors think similar to my experiences, and some who don't.

Case Report: Florence Nightingale's Fever. (23 December). BMJ 1995; 311: 1697.

Decisions Decisions: Getting Answers to Life's Challenges: Volume 1 Getting Started. By Haneefa Mateen (2023).

Decisions Decisions: Getting Answers to Life's Challenges: Volume 2 Returning. By Haneefa Mateen (2023).

Florence Nightingale: The Case for Brucellosis. (2019) Health. Steemit.com

Florence Nightingale's Long COVID. Sarah L. Mauer. (24 November 2021). Nineteenth-Century Context. Taylor and Francis online. https://doi.org/10.1080/08905495.2021.1987776

Holistic Tarot: An Integrative Approach to Using Tarot for Personal Growth. By Ben Bell Wen (2015). Berkeley, CA: North Atlantic Books.

I Ching: A New Interpretation for Modern Times. By Sam Reifler (1974).

I Ching: The Tao of Drumming. By Michael Drake. (1991). Talking Drum Publications. (paperback). Random House Publishing Group. (e-book).

I Ching Praxis: Forty Years of Practical Insights into the I Ching. By Ra Un Nefer Amen (2014). Khamit Media Trans Visions, Inc.

Left to Tell: Discovering God Amidst the Rwandan Holocaust By Immaculee Ilibagiza. (2006). Hay House.

Light Emerging: The Journey of Personal Healing. By Barbara Ann Brennan. (1993). Bantam Books.

Love, Medicine, and Miracles: Lessons Learned about Self-Healing from a Surgeon's Experiences with Exceptional Patients. By Bernie Sigel M.D. (1990). HarperPerennial.

Mary Magdalene Revealed: The First Apostle, Her Feminist Gospel, and the Christianity We Haven't Tried. By Meggan Waterson. (2019). Hay House.

Metu Neter Cards. By Ra Un Nefer Amen (1990). New York, Khamit Corporation.

Metu Neter Vol. 1: The Great Oracle of Tehuti and the Egyptian System of Spiritual Cultivation. By Ra Un Nefer Amen (1990). New York, Khamit Corporation.

Mind Over Matter: Scientific Proof That You Can Heal Yourself. By Lissa Rankin, M.D. (2013). Hay House.

Mother God: The Feminine Principle to Our Creator. By Sylvia Browne. (2004). Hay House.

Mother's Love from Beyond: A Healing Journey of Grief and Loss: A Memoir. By Haneefa Mateen. (2021).

Mystical Traveler: How to Advance to a Higher Level of Spirituality. By Sylvia Browne. (2008). Hay

Our Lady of Kibeho: Mary Speaks to the World from the Heart of Africa. By Immaculee Ilibagiza. (2008). Hay House.

Pain, Pain, Go Away. By Vicky Uhland. (Winter 2015-2016). Momentum. National Multiple Sclerosis Society.

Physicians' Untold Stories: Miraculous Experiences Doctors are Hesitant to Share With Their Patients, or Anyone! By Scott J. Kolbaba, M.D. with 26 other Physicians (2016).

Race, Gender and Imperialism in the Wonderful Adventures of Mrs. Seacole in Many Lands. C. Janneck, G. Cypher, A. Rivera, K. Schommer, and O. Hayes. Women in the world global connections and British women's travel writing 1780–1860. Https://britishwomentravelwriters.wordpress.com

Return of the Rishi. By Deepak Chopra. (1991). HarperOne.

Sacred Path Cards: The Discovery of Self through Native Teachings. By Jamie Sams (1990). New York: HarperCollins Publishers.

Sacred Path Workbook: New Teachings and Tools to Illuminate Your Personal Journey. By Jamie Sams (1991). New York: HarperCollins Publishers.

Soul's Perfection: Journey of the Soul series, Book 2. Sylvia Browne. (2000). Hay House.

The Astrology of I Ching. (1976, 1993). By W. K. Chu and W. A. Sherrill. Penguin Books.

The Forgotten Child of Zimbabwe. By Debra Chidaka Akue (2017). Christian Faith Publishing.

The I Ching or Book of Changes. By Richard Wilhelm and Cary Baynes. (1950). Princeton University Press.

The Illustrated I Ching Workbook. R. L. Wing. (1987). Aquarian Press.

The Medical I Ching: Oracle of the Healer Within. By Miki Shima. (1992, 2011). Blue Poppy Press.

Warm Up to Winter. By Aviva Patz. Winter 2015-2016). Momentum. National Multiple Sclerosis Society.

Wonderful Adventures of Mrs. Seacole in Many Lands. By Mary Seacole. (1857). London. James Blackwood Paternoster Row.

Author's Bio

Haneefa Mateen has a wealth of life experiences and knowledge from exploring healing methods for mind, body and soul. A natural teacher, healer, and artist she shares more of her wisdom. Her books are accessible, easy on the eyes, in large print format.

She has an associate's degree in registered nursing, bachelor's in International Studies, master's in Rehabilitation Counseling, and a doctorate in Clinical Psychology. She currently does spiritually integrated therapy and healing, and is active in

African American community cultural events.

www.ingramcontent.com/pod-product-compliance
Lightning Source LLC
Chambersburg PA
CBHW020523080526
44583CB00013B/716